DATE DUE

MR 22 '94			

DEMCO 38-297

DRUGGED ATHLETES

THE CRISIS IN AMERICAN SPORTS

by Jonathan Harris

FOUR WINDS PRESS
NEW YORK

Macmillan books are available at special discounts for bulk
purchases for sales promotions, premiums, fund-raising,
or educational use. Special editions or book excerpts
can also be created to specification. For details, contact:
Special Sales Director
Macmillan Publishing Company
866 Third Avenue, New York, NY 10022

Macmillan Publishing Company
866 Third Avenue, New York, NY 10022
Collier Macmillan Canada, Inc.
First Edition
Printed in the United States of America

10   9   8   7   6   5   4

The text of this book is set in 12-point Times Roman.

Library of Congress Cataloging-in-Publication Data
Harris, Jonathan.   Drugged athletes.
Bibliography: p.   Includes index.
Summary: Examines the widespread pattern of drug
abuse in sports at all levels.
1. Doping in sports—Juvenile literature.
2. Athletes—Drug use—Juvenile literature.
[1. Athletes—Drug use. 2. Drug abuse]   I. Title.
RC1230.H37   1987   364.1'77   86-29396
ISBN 0-02-742740-4

For Martha
with love and admiration
ever growing

CONTENTS

ACKNOWLEDGMENTS

Sports people ranging from junior high school athletes to high-level administrators contributed to the content of this book. In personal interviews, in lengthy telephone discussions, in detailed letters, they gave generously of their time, their specialized knowledge, and their experience. But the sensitive nature of the subject compelled some to request anonymity. The author is grateful to them all, and wishes to express his appreciation publicly to:

Ruth M. Berkey, assistant executive director, National Collegiate Athletic Association; Joe Browne, director of communications, National Football League; Carl Eller, former All-Pro defensive end, now a National Football League drug consultant, developer of the NFL's Chemical Dependency and Awareness Training Program; Donald M. Fehr, executive director, Major League Baseball Players' Association; Thomas M. Griffin, manager, education and health promotion services, Hazelden Foundation; Michael D. Hall, former athletic director, now principal, Anderson High School, Cincinnati, Ohio, chief developer of the Drug Enforcement Administration's model high school drug abuse prevention program; Mark Murphy, assistant to the executive director, National Football League Players Association; Martha O'Leary, president, Nassau County Association of School-Based Drug Prevention Specialists; Ernie Parker, former Denver Broncos defensive back, now drug counselor, Center for the Study of Sports in Society;

Lynn Sitrin, director, Bureau of Prevention, New York State Division of Substance Abuse Services; David J. Stern, commissioner, National Basketball Association; Dr. Robert O. Voy, director, Division of Sports Medicine and Science, United States Olympic Committee; John A. Ziegler, Jr., president, National Hockey League.

A NOTE ON GENDER

Women play an increasingly impressive role in sports today. Larger numbers compete than ever before. They have won acceptance in sports that were virtually closed to them not long ago. Their achievements keep rising to ever higher levels.

Female athletes have not escaped the drug and alcohol abuse problems that afflict their male colleagues. Certain sections of this book deal specifically with these problems as they affect women.

But the vast majority of documented cases of drug and alcohol abuse involve male athletes. The male pronoun has therefore been used throughout to denote athletes of both sexes, except in those sections focusing on women's special problems. There was no other way to keep the book readable.

DRUGGED ATHLETES

THE CRISIS IN AMERICAN SPORTS

1

THE DRUG MENACE— HOW BIG, HOW REAL?

By the time they have made the pros, most athletes have been given so many pills, salves, injections and potions, by amateur and pro coaches, doctors and trainers, to pick them up, cool them out, kill pain, enhance performance, reduce inflammation and erase anxiety, that there isn't much they won't sniff, spread, stick in or swallow to get bigger or smaller, or to feel goooood.—Robert Lipsyte, The Nation, *May 25, 1985*

Drugs to increase strength, speed, accuracy. Drugs to make athletes more aggressive. Drugs to mask pain. Drugs to relax overstrained muscles. Drugs to relieve mental stress. Drugs for sheer pleasure. Drugs to improve performance in any way that seems even remotely possible.

Athletes have sought out and used such drugs for at least a century and probably much longer. But they have never used drugs in such quantities as they do today.

American athletes stand at or close to the pinnacle of excellence in many sports. Yet they almost certainly abuse drugs as much as any athletes in the world—and possibly more.

Athletes are not unique in abusing drugs and liquor. Their behavior is shaped by the society that surrounds them. And the statistics on drug abuse in American society today are mind-boggling.

1

Americans now spend between $80 billion and $120 billion a year on illegal drugs—mainly marijuana, hashish, heroin, cocaine, amphetamines, and other pills of various kinds. Drug use has infected nearly every occupation. Even people entrusted with the safety of the public, such as airline pilots, flight attendants, doctors, nurses, police officers, fire fighters, bus drivers, train engineers, and nuclear plant workers, have become addicted.

Marijuana remains the most popular drug, with an estimated 20 to 30 million users. About 10 percent of these smoke an average of five "joints" a day. The marijuana crop is the nation's second largest, after corn.

Alcoholic drinks rank highest among the legal drugs—legal for adults, that is. Out of a total population of 240 million Americans, more than 100 million use alcohol. One in ten drinkers is an alcoholic. Some 80 percent of these alcoholics come from families in which one or both parents were alcoholics.

In ever-mounting numbers, young people, too, are abusing alcohol. Ruth Berkey, assistant executive director of the National Collegiate Athletic Association (NCAA), says, "Alcohol is by far the drug of choice among college athletes." The National Clearinghouse for Alcohol Information reported in 1984 that 75 percent of teenagers drink. About 15 percent are considered heavy drinkers.

A *Family Circle* magazine survey published in the fall of 1985 reported even higher percentages. One in five high school students admitted to getting drunk at least once a week. Even more disturbing, more than 500,000 ten- to thirteen-year-olds confessed to the same habit.

A similar pattern applies to cocaine. The Drug Enforcement Administration has estimated that the amount of cocaine consumed in the United States every year now totals a massive 95 metric tons (212,800 pounds). From 10 to 20 million Americans are thought to be occasional users. Half a million to a million are addicts who use it every day. On any given day, about 5,000 people try cocaine for the first time.

Dr. Mark S. Gold, founder of the national cocaine hot line, with its memorable phone number 800-COCAINE, did a random survey of five hundred callers. All had severe cocaine problems. One out of three was a woman. Eighty-five percent were white. Most were well educated, with relatively high incomes.

According to the Center for Disease Control, the number of cocaine abusers admitted to federally funded treatment programs has more than tripled since 1977.

And young people are among the growing number of cocaine users. Half a million high-schoolers admitted using it, while 100,000 sixth- to eighth-graders did. Many others were undoubtedly too ashamed or afraid to acknowledge their habit. The true figures are probably higher.

"Coke" long ago surpassed heroin as the illegal hard drug of choice. As the quantities smuggled into the United States have increased, the price has come down considerably—from $125 a gram only four years ago to between $50 and $70 in 1986. That fact partly explains its growing use by young people.

But even with this gradual drop in price, coke remains an expensive indulgence. Young abusers most commonly obtain the money they need for coke by stealing from their parents or their peers, or by dealing drugs. An unknown number of teenage girls have turned to prostitution to support their coke habit.

- Marijuana is the one drug whose abuse by teenagers has declined in recent years. While nearly 11 percent of all high school seniors were smoking "pot" daily in 1978, only 5 percent were doing so in 1985.

The drug had certainly not become hard to get. High school seniors were surveyed in the early 1980s as to which drugs they found easily available at or around their schools. Nearly 90 percent said they could easily "cop" marijuana. Over 60 percent reported the same about amphetamines, while the figure for cocaine was nearly 48 percent.

MEASURING THE DRUG MENACE

Detailed studies of drug abuse among athletes were begun only recently. The first nationwide survey of college athletes was ordered by the National Collegiate Athletic Association in August 1983. Medical researchers at Michigan State University's College of Human Medicine conducted the actual investigation, collecting responses from slightly more than 2,000 student athletes. The study took about a year to complete.

The survey's questions about drinking yielded dramatic results. No fewer than 82 percent of the athletes reported recent, regular use of alcohol. Interestingly, the figures for male and female athletes were roughly equal. The comparable figure for 18- to 25-year-old nonathletes, according to an earlier study by the National Institute of Drug Abuse, was 67 percent.

The survey also produced troubling responses covering abuse of marijuana and hashish. Of the athletes who admitted using these drugs, nearly a quarter had done so 40 or more times during the previous year. Ten percent had used them more than 20 times, and 15 percent more than 10 times. Most users smoked no more than one or two joints each time.

Cocaine users, too, were asked how frequently they indulged. Slightly more than half said they had used it 5 times or less during the previous year. A roughly equal number had used the drug from as few as 6 to as many as 40 times or more.

Similar questions about amphetamines brought answers indicating abuse rates approximately equal to those for cocaine.

The most surprising results were those related to anabolic steroids, the highly controversial drugs used to build strength and endurance. Only 4 percent of the athletes said they used steroids. This figure is far below that reported by other researchers since 1983.

Some experts believe that no formal survey can ever reflect the full truth about illegal drugs. The true level of drug abuse by athletes is thought to be higher than has been officially reported, since athletes—who face possible suspension or expulsion from sports for abuse of illegal drugs—are often reluctant to admit it. While the athletes in the Michigan State study were assured that their identities would be shielded, investigators had to admit that responses to the survey might not be entirely accurate.

Distressing responses were obtained when the athletes were asked at what age level they had started using drugs.

Nearly a quarter had started abusing alcohol in junior high school or even before. About two-thirds began drinking in high school. Some 58 percent reported smoking their first joints—and trying their first amphetamines—in high school. The high school figure for starting on cocaine was 42 percent.

The Michigan survey tried to determine how much drug abuse went on in each of the most popular sports. Surprisingly, cocaine abuse turned out to be highest in men's tennis. Baseball, football, and basketball ranked close behind, in that order. Track athletes used the drug to a considerably lesser extent. The results for marijuana and hashish were similar. An unexpected finding showed that female swimmers used drugs and alcohol considerably more than women in other sports.

The survey results left at least one disputed question unresolved: Do athletes drink and abuse drugs more than other people? In some drug categories, the figures showing either recent or continuing abuse by athletes were higher than those for the general population. In others, they were about the same.

The NCAA's Ruth Berkey argued in a letter to the author that athletes "are conscious of their physical well-being in a more intense fashion than their peers." It seemed logical to her that "athletes abuse drugs and alcohol less than nonathletes."

Other representatives of the sports establishment agreed. In separate interviews with the author, David J. Stern of the National Basketball Association (NBA) and Mark Murphy of the National Football League (NFL) Players Association challenged the idea that athletes are any more likely to abuse drugs or alcohol than the general public. Murphy did admit that some of the "extra stresses" of big-time sports competition might drive players to seek relief in narcotics.

As an example of these extra stresses, Murphy noted that the intensity of a game stimulates players to a special kind of high. Some hate to come down afterward. They take drugs to maintain the high.

The seasonal nature of many sports brings on still another kind of stress. During the long off-season, players often find it hard to remain "up," to stay in shape, to live healthy and disciplined lives. Drugs and drinking are ways of evading the problem.

Queried about Olympic athletes, U.S. Olympic Committee sports medicine specialist Dr. Robert O. Voy admitted that their drug-taking and drinking habits have never been measured. But Dr. Voy added, "In my opinion, the percentages are very high." They were not high enough, however, to convince him that athletes abuse drugs or alcohol more than nonathletes. "They are just more visible to the public," he wrote, "similar to others in our society that have celebrity status and a lot of money to spend."

Lynn Sitrin, director of the Bureau of Prevention of the New York State Division of Substance Abuse Services, explained to the author why comparisons between athletes and the general population could not be precise. Some groups in the general population use drugs more than others. Accurate comparisons could be made only between athletes and specific groups whose drug and drinking habits had been measured. No one has yet gathered the data needed for such comparisons.

Whatever the final truth may turn out to be about the scope of drug abuse by athletes, it is clear that the public has strong negative views of it. A *Sports Illustrated* poll published in June 1986 showed that 86 percent of Americans believe professional athletes use drugs. Nearly three out of four people favor having athletes submit to random tests. Pro football was thought to have the most serious problem, with baseball second and basketball third.

BIG-LEAGUE ADDICTS

Drug and alcohol abuse among athletes is at its worst among the professionals. Baseball fans in particular have been shocked by a long series of revelations. Since 1980, at least thirty-five major-league players have admitted to drug-related offenses, or have been arrested or convicted. Many more have had to enter treatment centers for detoxification and rehabilitation. Nearly all of the twenty-six major-league teams have been affected. In at least four cases, drug dealers or couriers had easy access to baseball clubhouses and made sales there.

The dealers' persistence has created problems throughout professional sports. "When we took road trips," says former Cleveland Browns coach Sam Rutigliano, "we found out that drug dealers were following us in the next plane . . . and that they had reservations at our hotel."

Some baseball officials have claimed that drug problems peaked in the early 1980s and are now declining. Baseball commissioner Peter Ueberroth differs sharply. He stated in 1985 that drug abuse in baseball was "greater" than ever, and was in fact the most urgent problem facing the sport.

Baseball players interviewed by the Federal Bureau of Investigation have asserted that 40 to 50 percent are currently using drugs. In one exceptional case in Kansas City, three members of the Kansas City Royals were convicted in 1982 and 1983, and each served three months in jail for possession of illegal drugs. The baseball commissioner suspended all of them for a full year.

Seven players testifying in a series of trials of drug dealers held in Pittsburgh in the fall of 1985 admitted to purchasing, using, and sharing cocaine. Unlike those in the Kansas City case, these men were granted immunity from prosecution in exchange for testimony that helped to convict the dealers. They did, however, have to submit to the embarrassment of being publicly derided as "junkies" and "hero-criminals" by a defense lawyer. Their testimony implicated twenty other players, including some of the top stars in both leagues.

"Not since the infamous Black Sox scandal [of 1919]," wrote Michael Goodwin of the *New York Times,* "had baseball been so publicly humiliated, and even then the stain did not touch as many big names as it did in Pittsburgh."

Federal Judge Gustave Diamond, who presided at one of the trials, said afterward that it had shown millions of baseball fans that "their idols have feet of clay." But he added that the public had "learned of the evils of fooling around with drugs in a way that no advertising campaign could have accomplished."

As soon as the trials were over, baseball commissioner Peter Ueberroth began a series of hearings with the players who had either testified or had been named as drug abusers. His aim was to determine how deeply involved each of them was, what their attitudes were, and what action he should take.

Ueberroth could have suspended them all, but he decided against that. The hearings had convinced him that the players were not all equally guilty. "The vast majority," he believed, were remorseful. "If they were sincere about what they told me, that they felt they could help and even had an obligation to help, then don't suspend them for a single day." Ueberroth felt it was better "to let them be a positive force, on and off the field."

Seven players were ordered to donate 10 percent of their 1986 salaries to drug-prevention programs, perform 100 hours of community service in drug programs, and undergo random drug tests for the rest of their playing careers. Any who refused would be suspended for a year.

For some of the players, the enforced "donation" actually constituted a heavy fine. Keith Hernandez of the Mets, for example, earned more than a million dollars in 1986. His 10 percent donation amounted to about $135,000.

Ueberroth ordered four others to donate 5 percent of their salaries and 50 hours of community service. They, too, would be tested randomly until they left baseball. Their alternative was a 60-day suspension. Ten players had only to submit to testing.

In the National Basketball Association, officials estimate that from 40 to 75 percent of the players use coke. One in ten is thought to be "freebasing."

The infection runs equally deep in the National Football League. One investigative reporter estimated that as many as 50 percent of the NFL's 1,372 players have taken cocaine. More than 20 percent were hard-core addicts. On average, about ten players in each team were hooked on the drug.

NFL commissioner Pete Rozelle had for some years downplayed drug use among the players. By the mid-1980s the evidence could no longer be ignored. Forty-three players had been treated for drug or alcohol abuse in the off-season. Seven others had been indicted on drug charges.

In September 1983 Rozelle had to suspend four players who had been convicted of drug offenses. The commissioner publicly acknowledged that the NFL's drug problem "may be a bigger one than [that of] society as a whole." Further study of the problem convinced Rozelle that, as he told a TV interviewer in 1985, "The drug issue is the biggest concern of the fans. They want to have a clean sport. . . ."

Super Bowl XX had hardly ended in January 1986 when the losing team's coach, Raymond Berry of the New England Patriots, went public with the admission that drug involvements had bedeviled his team for an entire year. Berry estimated that a dozen players, including four starters, were affected. Immediately afterward, the team voted to accept a voluntary drug-testing program, becoming the first in the NFL to do so.

At least half a dozen NFL teams have ridden the same roller coaster. With as many as six members of a single team hooked on coke, they have sunk from contention for championships to the cellar.

In baseball, the Pittsburgh Pirates suffered a similar fate. World champions one year, they fell to the bottom of the National League the next. Drug dealers had gained access to their clubhouse.

The National Hockey League may be an exception. In a forcefully phrased letter to me, league president John A. Ziegler, Jr., declared that drug abuse is less of a problem among pro hockey players than among other athletes. "Our rules are simple," Ziegler wrote. "If you want to use illegal drugs, get out of hockey." His policy is "firm and stern punishment." He is convinced that it deters the players from getting into the drug scene.

Ziegler had earlier explained hockey's seeming immunity to the drug crisis in a statement to the press. He had said it was at least partly due to "the dedication it takes to achieve the skill level it takes to be in the NHL." But he emphasized the league's tough antidrug policy above all.

There have been two widely publicized cases of drug involvement affecting NHL players. They demonstrate just how tough the policy is.

One happened back in 1978. New York Rangers player Don Murdoch had been arrested and pleaded guilty to possession of cocaine. Murdoch insisted that the drug was not even his, but had come into his possession through some mistake. Ziegler believed him, but still fined him $500 and suspended him for the entire 1978–1979 season (later reduced to a forty-game suspension).

In 1984, Montreal player Ric Nattress was convicted for possession of hashish. The fact that the incident had occurred before he was in the NHL made no difference. He, too, was suspended for forty games.

The NHL has no plans to introduce a drug-treatment program like that in effect in some other leagues. Ziegler put it this way: "Rehabilitation is not a League responsibility. The member clubs may wish to assist in rehabilitation and treatment; however, this will have no effect on the discipline to be imposed."

THE PERFORMANCE BOOSTERS

Alcohol, cocaine, and other "street" drugs are obviously not the only drugs abused by athletes, nor are they the most widely used, either. Surpassing them by far are drugs that athletes believe will enhance their strength and energy. Most common are the amphetamines, variously referred to as "pep pills," "uppers," "greenies," "beans," or by many other names. The anabolic steroids run these a close second.

Players in several sports have described how coaches and trainers routinely distribute pep pills and steroids to team members—even in junior high and high schools. Back in 1970, Paul Lowe, formerly an All-Pro running back with the San Diego Chargers, testified about this before the Subcommittee on Drug Abuse and Alcoholism of the California State Legislature. "We had to take [steroids] at lunchtime," Lowe said. "[The trainer] would put them on a little saucer and prescribed for us to take them, and if not he would suggest there might be a fine."

Dave Meggysey, former star of the NFL's St. Louis Cardinals, testified that the team's trainer "had what amounted to a drugstore down in his training room. The drug cabinets were open and could be used by any player."

The situation was not very different in baseball. John Milner played for several major-league teams in the 1970s and early 1980s. He testified in one of the 1985 trials that he was regularly supplied with amphetamines. "When I came into the clubhouse," Milner said, "[they] would be in my locker."

Milner shocked the courtroom by alleging that he had even seen "red juice," an illegal mixture of amphetamines and fruit juice, in the locker belonging to venerable Hall of Famer Willie Mays. Milner admitted that he had never seen Mays actually drink the stuff. Mays later claimed he did not remember having it.

"[Athletes] have far more access to drugs than most of us," *Sports Illustrated* writer Bill Gilbert explained:

> They do not have to stand around in waiting rooms, at pharmacy counters, or on street corners for their fixes. Drugs are brought to them, and usually provided free of charge. The athlete gets free professional advice from physicians and assisting trainers as to what drugs to take, and when, and how."

An authoritative judgment as to where athletes get drugs came from the U.S. Olympic Committee's Dr. Voy. He believes that physicians in general, not only team physicians, supply approximately 40 percent. Another 40 percent comes from the black market. The remaining 20 percent "is provided from various sources, trainers, pharmacists, friends, etc."

The steroids have long been favored among athletes in the strength sports, such as weightlifting, hammer throwing, and shotputting. These drugs have been officially banned in international competition since 1967, and athletes have been required to undergo testing for them for years. Up to the late 1970s, however, there had been only occasional disqualifications. In the 1968 Olympics, for example, twenty track and field athletes and weightlifters were surveyed. Nineteen admitted taking steroids to prepare. None was barred from the games.

But by the early 1980s, the tests had reached a degree of refinement never approached before. Increasing numbers of athletes were discovered to be using drugs and were barred from competition. Athletes and their supporters sought desperately for new substances that the tests would not detect.

Soviet and East European athletes are notorious for their use and often sophisticated concealment of banned drugs. A popular story at the 1976 Olympics concerned the abnormally deep voices of the East German women swimmers (steroids tend to have this effect on women). They had won an astonishing number of races. When their coach was asked about their voices, he could only reply, "We have come here to swim, not to sing."

Other countries have been equally guilty. In Britain, for example, the *Sunday Times* of London reported early in 1985 that about six out of ten British track and field athletes take illegal drugs regularly.

Reports of performance-enhancing drug use date from as early as the 1860s. Substances tried in European competitions of that era included sugar tablets soaked in ether, caffeine tablets, oxygen, cocaine, heroin, strychnine, and brandy. A big dose of the last two was taken by Tom Hicks, winner of the marathon at the 1904 Olympics in St. Louis.

He collapsed after crossing the finish line, and it required the combined efforts of four doctors to revive him.

The 1960 Olympics were the first and, so far, the only ones to be scarred by the deaths of athletes from drug abuse. A Danish cyclist who had taken nicotinic acid and amphetamines was the first victim. The second was an American 400-meter hurdler, who had taken heroin.

Athletes' drug dependence has increased vastly since those days. That fact may increase the likelihood of drug-related deaths. It is certainly raising the number of prematurely burnt-out athletes.

THE POWER OF PUBLIC OPINION

Public reactions to sports drugs scandals have thus far been surprisingly uncritical. A September 1985 poll by *New York Newsday* showed that only one-third of those surveyed thought less of the baseball players revealed to be cocaine addicts. Well over half did not think the athletes should be disciplined for past drug use. About two-thirds did feel that the players should be required to take urine tests to make sure they are not using drugs.

Attendance at ball parks, and at football and basketball games, has seemed unaffected. At the very time when the baseball drug revelations were making the headlines, the major leagues signed a new TV contract that boosted their revenue to an astronomical $1.2 billion.

But some TV ratings for sportscasts were dropping. Particularly affected was ABC-TV's "Monday Night Football," long rated among TV's top ten. Sportscaster Howard Cosell was one of the show's stars for fourteen years. In his recent best-selling memoir *I Never Played the Game*, Cosell blamed the fans' "disillusionment with coke-snorting players" as a major cause of the show's declining popularity.

"The fans obviously care," said Dr. Ronald Stern, a psychotherapist who is president and founder of an antidrug group called Sports Against Substance Abuse. "But they are tired of caring."

Athletes, coaches, trainers, sports officials, fans—all those even remotely connected with sports—are watching the tide of public opinion closely. If or when it shifts, public anger and disgust may eventually compel forceful action to drive drug abuse out of sports. If that fails, many fans may simply walk away from the sports they love.

Why? The fans ask. Why do so many of our most idolized athletes let themselves get hooked? A study of individual examples reveals that the reasons are as subtle and complex as human nature itself.

2

PROFILES OF DRUG-ABUSER ATHLETES

For some athletes, the drug habit has brought shame and despair and expulsion from sports. Others have triumphed over addiction and have proudly returned to competition. And still others have avoided any serious entanglement with drugs.

There is no simple way to predict which athletes will make it and which will not. These men and women are as complicated a group of human beings as any in society.

What factors make the difference between overcoming the habit and being overcome by it? Case histories supply helpful clues.

FOUR WHO DIDN'T MAKE IT

There are three things that can happen to you when you get hooked on drugs. One is go to jail. Another is to get rehabilitated. The third is death. It will kill you. Believe me, it will kill you dead.

The speaker is former basketball superstar John Drew. He played eight seasons for the Atlanta Hawks. He was drug-free for the first three. His playing rivaled the NBA's best. Drew was averaging nearly 25 points a game. Then, after a game in Portland, Oregon, a man came up and introduced himself. "He was the kind of a guy," says Drew, "who goes to all the teams and finds out who does drugs."

The guy offered Drew some cocaine. Drew tried it and liked it. It was all downhill from that point.

Drew was similar to many young athletes dazzled by sudden wealth. When the Hawks first drafted him, he signed a five-year contract for $780,000 plus a $40,000 bonus. "For a kid who never had a hundred dollars in his pocket," said Drew, "that was a helluva jump."

He was one of five boys in a poor, rural Alabama family. Now barely into his twenties, he had money enough for anything—even a thing as expensive as coke.

Drew was soon using so much of the drug that his behavior changed dramatically. "He was fidgety," says a longtime girlfriend, and he

> always had somewhere to go. When he got worse, we couldn't even go to a movie. He'd have to get up three or four times, said he had to make a phone call. Everything was always rush, rush, rush.

Amazingly, Drew was still able to play top-notch basketball. He averaged 19.5 points in the 1979–1980 season, even though he had already started freebasing.

Drew's addiction could not be kept secret for long. The Hawks management soon learned of it and tried to help. Three times they sent him to a twenty-eight-day detoxification program in Charleston, South Carolina. But such programs can succeed only when the patient has a real desire to break the habit. Drew resisted stubbornly. Finally, the Hawks traded him to the Utah Jazz.

Drew missed practices, missed a game, missed a team plane. At the beginning of the 1982–1983 season, Jazz coach Frank Layden got Drew enrolled in an intensive eight-week treatment program in Baltimore. It was a tough, no-frills program, but Drew stuck it out. By the time it was over he seemed at long last to have kicked his five-year habit. He was clean for many months.

But the temptation proved too great. Drew went back on the drug. The Jazz waived him in the middle of the 1984–1985 season. No other team would touch him.

Drew was not only out of a job, he was broke—despite years with a six-figure income. Most of his money had gone for coke and high living. He tried to pass several checks for which he had no funds and was arrested.

The judge ordered him held in the Salt Lake City jail on $10,000 bail. Drew could not raise anything near that amount. He turned to his former team for help. The Jazz management, after some painful soul-searching, refused to pay Drew's bail.

"We feel," said Jazz president David Checketts, "like we traveled the second mile with John, and we wish him the best." Drew eventually got a light sentence, including a ninety-day treatment program at a Salt Lake City hospital. When he came out, Coach Layden told him the Jazz would never rehire him. The best Drew could do was to find a spot with a Continental Basketball Association team, the Wyoming Wildcatters.

Los Angeles Dodgers pitcher Steve Howe suffered a fate that was similar in some ways, though he managed to stay out of jail. Back in 1981 he had been voted the National League's Rookie of the Year. Then he, too, got hooked on coke. Within a period of seven months in 1983, he had to go into treatment for addiction two separate times. The following year, when his pattern of drug abuse continued, baseball commissioner Bowie Kuhn suspended him for the entire season. Howe went through still another rehabilitation program. The Dodgers welcomed the talented lefthander back for the 1985 season.

But early that summer Howe disappeared for several days. The coke habit had proved too strong for him. The Dodgers released him.

A few weeks later the Minnesota Twins decided to take a chance on Howe. He seemed fine for a while. He even appeared on ABC-TV's "Nightline" to discuss baseball's drug problems. But he disappeared again the next day and did not show up for three days. When he finally did surface, Howe admitted he'd been on the drug again.

The Twins dropped him. Howe eventually found a place in the minor leagues, pitching for the San Jose Bees. It didn't last long. In the summer of 1986, another drug test turned out positive. For what seemed the final time, Steve Howe was out of baseball.

Even more tragic is the case of Eugene "Mercury" Morris, once a razzle-dazzle running back for the Miami Dolphins. Morris helped power the Dolphins in three successive Super Bowl games in the mid-1970s. Then he suffered a broken neck near the end of the 1973 season. The injury was not diagnosed properly until later. It caused agonizing headaches.

About that time, Morris began to use cocaine. It was not hard to find in Miami, which is one of the major ports of entry for illegal drugs. "I attracted lots of strange people,"

Morris told *Inside Sports* magazine, "hustlers, Mafia guys, dope dealers, gamblers. . . ." Morris was not alone; several of his teammates were on coke, too.

Doctors warned Morris before the 1977 season that his injury might lead to paralysis if he kept playing. He had no choice but to retire. Like many dedicated athletes, he was totally unprepared for life outside of sports. "In pro football," he recalled, "you know what you are going to be doing almost every week of the year. I never learned how to be quarterback of my own life."

Morris had a neck operation in 1980, but the headaches persisted. "Drugs were a frequent refuge. I'd go in spurts of three or four days of smoking marijuana and freebasing coke, starting in 1979." His personal life started to fall apart, and his debts started to mount.

In mid-1982, Morris got in on what looked like a profitable deal. If he could line up a buyer for 2 kilos (4.4 pounds) of cocaine with a dealer, he'd earn an $8,000 commission. After a series of parking-lot meetings and phone calls, the deal was set. Unfortunately for Morris, the buyer turned out to be an undercover agent for the Florida Department of Law Enforcement.

Morris was convicted of cocaine trafficking, conspiracy to sell cocaine, and two counts of possession. Because he was so well known and had been so widely admired by youngsters all over the country, the judge felt that Morris should be made an example. She dealt out the maximum sentence: twenty years in prison.

Mercury Morris might have gotten off more lightly by turning in the drug abusers among his teammates and the many dealers he knew. Right or wrong, he could not bring himself to do that.

Morris got a big break in March 1986, when the Florida Supreme Court ordered a new trial for him. The court said that evidence had been improperly excluded from the original trial. It might have shown that the police had illegally entrapped Morris into making the cocaine deal.

The Florida prosecutors were not optimistic about a second trial. They agreed to a deal under which Morris was allowed to enter a new plea of "no contest" to the charges. On June 12, 1986, after three and a half years in prison, Morris was a free man.

The case of New Jersey Nets guard Micheal Ray Richardson shows how unpredictable abuser-athletes can be. He has been on and off cocaine four times in three years.

Richardson was named the National Basketball Association's comeback player of the year in May 1985. He had played in eighty-two games that season, averaging 20.1 points and leading the league in steals. During his five years in the NBA, Richardson had been an All-Star three times.

Yet in the 1983–1984 season Richardson had been able to play in only forty-eight games. He was then recovering from a cocaine habit that had been building for at least three years. It had very nearly destroyed both his athletic talent and his personal life. His wife of eight years was suing for divorce and custody of their only child. He was thousands of dollars in debt. At 28, Richardson was apparently finished as a player, as a husband, as a father.

As one of seven children, he had never gotten much

attention. His grades were low through his entire school career. Basketball was his one meaningful interest. It got him an athletic scholarship at the University of Montana.

Drafted by the New York Knicks in 1978, Richardson went through an experience like John Drew's. He got a four-year contract worth $909,000, plus a bonus of $149,000. The wild behavior that followed showed how ill-prepared he was to handle such sudden wealth. In the next five years he went through six agents, sixteen fancy cars, and a scary amount of cocaine.

Traded twice, Richardson wound up on the New Jersey Nets. That team's management knew of his problem but hoped to help him. He was persuaded to go into treatment. Twice he failed to complete the program.

At one point the Nets gave up on him and placed him on waivers. But Richardson pulled himself together. He stayed with his third rehabilitation program to the end. He then agreed to be tested for drugs four times a week.

For two years after that, Richardson passed every test. He was playing better than ever. In September 1985, when his contract expired, the Nets signed him to a rich new multiyear deal. He was now the team's playmaker.

Then, at the end of the year, after playing in 151 consecutive games, Richardson suddenly disappeared for three days. When he resurfaced, he admitted he had relapsed into cocaine. The Nets management once again referred him to a rehabilitation center, and the stricken player resumed the arduous comeback battle. "The biggest thing now is, as a team, we must lend support to him," said Nets coach Dave Wohl.

"I know I disappointed a lot of people," said Richardson when he returned after two and a half weeks in treatment. "I'd like to apologize to the players and the fans." Coach Wohl eased him back into action in gradual stages.

Richardson faced a rigorous aftercare program. He was required to attend three meetings a week with drug counselors. They are available in all the cities visited by NBA teams. For a full year, he would be tested after every counseling session. In addition, he had to attend a meeting of Cocaine Anonymous once each week and talk with the Los Angeles treatment center's drug counselor every day.

Richardson had scarcely begun on all this when he failed a urine test. This evidence left the NBA authorities with no choice. Richardson was banned from basketball, with the possibility that he might be allowed back after a minimum of two years.

THREE WHO CAME BACK

Not all athletes who fall victim to drugs or alcohol get driven out of sports. A substantial number have conquered their habits and have resumed their careers.

If anyone ever had a soul-wrenching childhood, New Orleans Saints nose tackle Tony Elliott did. His story was told by sportswriter Robert Lipsyte on a recent segment of the CBS-TV program "Sunday Morning."

When Elliott was 4½ years old, he saw his father stab his mother to death. The child was then shuttled from one foster home to another. When his father was released from prison, there was a squabble with an uncle who had been taking care of Elliott. The boy was once again a witness to murder, as his father killed his uncle.

Throughout his youth Elliott was, in his own words, "very insecure, very afraid of not being accepted." The tall, powerfully built youngster tried to make up for his inner fears by becoming "a show-off, a loudmouth, a bully." As Lipsyte noted during the TV show, Elliott also grew up to become "a drunk, and a criminal, and a drug addict."

"I honestly believe," says Elliott, "I would have been an addict if I had grown up with everything. It's part of me. I always showed addictive tendencies . . . starting with cigarettes, then drinking at thirteen, marijuana at sixteen, cocaine at nineteen. . . ."

Football was the one outlet that offered any possibility of a decent future. Elliott very nearly threw it away. He was All-American in high school and played for three different colleges. But he'd been drinking and using drugs since his early teens. As he wrote in the *New York Times,* "Boozing it up was supposed to be the sign of manhood for the young athlete. Now it's coke. . . . It's a status symbol. It gives you the illusion of power and masculinity. . . ."

During his high school years, Elliott had trouble bearing up under the pressures of his status as a star athlete. "Drugs and alcohol were a welcome relief. . . ."

The privileged treatment that top athletes get didn't help him to mature. "I had fewer chores, I had to study less, I got away with more in school, I never had to make plans. Everything was done for me. All I had to do was play [football]."

The situation was worse in college. "I was given money, apartments, cars. . . . Nobody doubted my intelligence. But nobody asked me to study." By his senior year, 1981, Elliott was heavily into cocaine.

When he got a $30,000 bonus for joining the Saints, Elliott spent most of it on freebasing the drug.

In the grip of cocaine addiction, Elliott was a constant source of trouble to the Saints coaches. He would break training, leave camp without permission, and commit petty crimes. His coke habit kept him broke.

Desperate for money at one point, Elliott decided to rob a drug dealer. All he had was "a rusty gun that wouldn't shoot." But the dealer came to the door brandishing a .357 Magnum. "Right then I really shook with fear," said Elliott. "That very night I checked myself in [to a halfway house for addicts], because I knew I was on my way to the graveyard."

The Saints had gone as far with him as they thought reasonable. In the middle of the 1984 football season, the team fired Elliott.

Elliott stayed at the halfway house for six months. At first he tried to fake his way through the drug-treatment program, but gradually the counselors' unyielding pressure for frankness and sincerity straightened him out. Elliott became a guest speaker at schools in the New Orleans area, helping young people trapped in the drug swamp.

There was only one way to get back into football. Elliott went to see NFL commissioner Pete Rozelle. That tough official's policy was never to readmit any player to the league who had been hooked on drugs. Elliott's honesty and his absolute determination to make good impressed Rozelle. He bent the rule, and the Saints welcomed Elliott back.

He has now been off drugs for nearly two years. The secret, he says, is "to take it one day at a time. . . . And if you make it, you have a sense of confidence like you never had before."

A different kind of addiction almost ruined Dodger pitcher Bob Welch. He was an alcoholic. As Welch says in his autobiography, he was raised in a "drinking family," where "weekends and holidays and family gatherings, good times and bad times" were all celebrated with booze. Welch was a chronic drinker by the time he got into high school.

> I loved getting drunk but I also drank because I was shy. Scared, really. Scared of girls. By the time I went to high school I'd discovered that if I had a few beers, I wouldn't be so awed of girls. . . .

Welch had a deep-seated need to please people and be liked. Baseball became his key to achieving it: "My whole personality was based on my being a star."

Like many high school kids, Welch tried several kinds of drugs. None ever gave him the relaxed, carefree feeling he got from booze. "I once tried a greenie, a pill that gives you energy, which was the last thing I needed. I couldn't get the ball anywhere near the plate and never tried that again."

In college, Welch quickly earned a reputation as an overpowering fastball pitcher. The Dodgers drafted him in 1978. Welch made a fine record in his first major-league season.

The young rookie was called in as relief pitcher in the ninth inning of the second game of the World Series. With one out, he faced fearsome Yankee batters Thurman Munson and Reggie Jackson. Welch got Munson to fly out. Then he struck Jackson out, ending the game in triumph.

Few major-league pitching careers have ever started more brilliantly. Welch should have been feeling secure. But his need to please never left him: "I was susceptible to every drink, every party, every banquet that was offered me. I didn't have the sense to say no."

By the 1979 season his habit was so bad that he even started taking drinks in the Dodger clubhouse during games, on days when he wasn't pitching. The problem became increasingly obvious to everyone around him as his behavior got more bizarre.

Loudly protesting that he was not an alcoholic, Welch was persuaded to enter an addiction treatment center called The Meadows, in Wickenburg, Arizona. He was a stubborn case, but their probing, no-nonsense techniques slowly and painfully brought him to face reality—and himself.

The Dodger organization supported him throughout, and he rejoined the team. He's been one of its most reliable pitchers ever since.

Welch is not "cured"; no alcoholic ever really is. He is a "recovering alcoholic," and he will be for the rest of his life. As he learned at The Meadows, the solution is to do it all—live life, play baseball, stay sober—one day at a time. Beyond that, no promises.

The cost of addiction varies. A heavy coke habit cost Don Reese, a former NFL defensive end, a year in jail followed later by another five-month jolt. It also cost him four years of football when he was at the peak of his powers.

Reese had been a star player at Jackson State. The Miami Dolphins drafted him as their first-round choice in 1976. But cocaine had already taken over his life, and the following year he was caught trying to sell the drug. Reese did a year in the Dade County, Florida, stockade.

When he got out, the New Orleans Saints picked him up. By 1979 he was leading the team in sacks and was named its most valuable defensive player. But his old coke habit soon mastered him again, and it was getting worse all the time.

The drug was costing him $400 a day. He was paying out another $250 a day in fines because he kept missing team meetings. After spending many thousands on the drug, he still owed dealers $30,000. Dealers had held guns on him more than once, threatening to kill him if he didn't pay.

Reese was close to suicide. More and more frequently he would black out mentally: "I was in a stupor much of the time. . . ." Plays I should have made easily I couldn't make at all. I was too strung out from the cocaine."

He found the situation in New Orleans a "horror show." Players were snorting coke in the locker rooms before games and at halftime. At night they'd roam the streets looking for a "connection." In 1980, the team lost fourteen straight.

Reese was traded again, this time to San Diego. Coke abuse was rife there, too. Desperate, in the spring of 1982 he announced that he was quitting the game he loved. Reese signed himself into a drug rehabilitation center.

Meanwhile he had been working closely with reporter John Underwood of *Sports Illustrated*. The result was a feature story that blew the lid off the drug situation in the NFL. "Cocaine," Reese told Underwood,

> can be found in quantity throughout the NFL. It's pushed on players, often from the edge of the practice field. Sometimes it's pushed by players. Prominent players. Just as it controlled me, it now controls and corrupts the game, because so many players are on it. To ignore this fact is to be short-sighted and stupid. To turn away from it the way the NFL does . . . is a crime.

When the story appeared, Reese was still on probation from his earlier conviction. His admission that he had been using coke since then was technically a violation of his probation. The judge sent him back to jail for another five months.

For three years after he was released, Reese tried to make a go of it as a sales executive. He stayed off coke, but he was totally bored. Then the Birmingham Stallions of the USFL decided to take a chance on him. In February 1985, at the age of 33, Reese was back where he belonged.

But besides blocking pass receivers and stopping running backs, he had an extra assignment. Younger teammates came to him and asked about his drug experience. "I'll tell them the whole story," he informed *USA Today*. "They're fascinated. They're all ears." Unfortunately for Reese, the USFL died in 1986 and his briefly revived career came to an apparently final end.

TWO WHO ESCAPED

There are, of course, many athletes who never get hooked on drugs. Some come perilously close to the drug scene, yet escape as if by some miracle.

Kareem Abdul-Jabbar of the Los Angeles Lakers, rated by many as basketball's all-time greatest, is one who admits he came close. In his autobiography, *Giant Steps,* Kareem says, "People had been trying to turn me on to marijuana since I was fifteen." He resisted for years.

When he finally did try it, it had no effect till the third "joint." After that he got high occasionally or smoked at parties. "I never found that marijuana did me any particular good. It didn't sharpen my hook shot or make my moves to the hoop even a fraction stronger."

Noting that Kareem led the Lakers to the NBA championship as recently as 1985, it is surprising to recall that he entered UCLA fully twenty years earlier. At that time LSD, the hallucinogenic chemical popularly known as "acid," was the rage among college students. He tried it, but found that he preferred real life to its sometimes frightening "trips." "What I ultimately learned . . .," he says, "was that I did not need to take acid."

Between college and the pros, Kareem even got into coke. One day, while driving under the drug's influence, he had a near-fatal accident. That was it for him; he never tried it again. "Habitual drug users," says Kareem, "have a hard time in the NBA. Most burn out in a year or two. People who [use coke] are losers. I play to win."

New York Times sportswriter Ira Berkow tells the moving story of another NBA great who has avoided the drug abyss.

His name is Isiah Thomas.

The youngest of seven boys, Thomas was raised by his mother in the slums of Chicago's West Side. Mrs. Thomas was a strong personality who struggled hard to keep him out of trouble. But it was his brothers who had the greatest influence on him. Considering their fate, the way he turned out is all the more amazing. Two of them became heroin addicts, another was a pimp, two others went to jail, and the last became chief of one of Chicago's most notorious street gangs, the Vice Lords.

But Thomas's brothers decided early that he would be different. They lectured him on the dangers of street life and took him on walking tours to point out the people and places he must watch out for. "They told me about the mistakes they had made, so that I wouldn't have to make them."

One brother, generally rated the family's best basketball player, won election to the All-City team. But he had severe problems in school and was eventually thrown out. According to Berkow, "He went into the streets and became a junkie. Isiah could see for himself the tortures his brother went through, and the suffering it caused his mother."

So it is Isiah Thomas who is having the brilliant basketball career his brother might have had. He never forgets the remarkable family that schooled him and watched over him and held him to the straight path.

WHO GETS HOOKED?

Psychiatrists, psychologists, social workers, and other mental health specialists have studied the inner worlds of the drug addict and the alcoholic in depth. They see a variety of factors as potential causes of addiction.

The addict's problems may stem from social, economic, and other environmental influences. Poverty, racial or ethnic discrimination, the strains and stresses of school or college, broken homes, peer pressures—a whole range of external factors may have shaped his personality. Even an individual raised in a well-to-do home may have suffered neglect, or been spoiled by overprotective and overgenerous parents.

In some cases biochemical factors are the root cause. Individuals from healthy backgrounds, with normal or even emotionally strong personalities, may become addicted because their bodies react to drugs or alcohol in abnormal ways. One pill, one snort, one drink can affect them more powerfully than other people.

Many specialists emphasize psychological weakness as the most common origin of addiction. Their conclusion is that the typical addict is, in the words of Dr. D. L. Bell, "a person with a seriously disturbed personality." He has difficulty enjoying life's normal satisfactions. He cannot cope with life's inevitable stresses.

Addicts' life histories vary widely, but there are similarities. Many have suffered childhoods marked by parental discord and separation. Often they were rejected, openly or in some disguised way, by their parents. And in a high number of cases, the parents were drinkers or drug addicts.

Individuals coming out of such backgrounds are extremely vulnerable when they meet others who encourage them to try drugs. In the case of professional athletes, this weakness is heightened by access to big money. Suddenly they can afford any self-indulgence that is offered.

What makes the difference? Why do the grinding stresses of competition drive some athletes but not all into the trap of addiction?

The difference lies in the pattern of psychological weakness that marks many athlete-addicts. They tend to be immature individuals who have trouble resisting impulses, who constantly seek immediate gratification. Their focus is always on the present moment, the here-and-now. Early in life they develop the habit of avoiding unpleasant realities rather than facing up to them.

Keith Hernandez, star first baseman for the Mets, is an interesting example. Testifying at a cocaine dealer's trial in 1985, he admitted heavy use of the drug in the early 1980s. Hernandez explained it this way in his published memoir of the 1985–1986 season:

> I think my basic personality may have led me to try cocaine. I was never one to look before I leaped, and this impulsiveness got me into trouble as a kid and in the minor leagues several times, and it did so again in 1980. It's this simple: the drug was there, I tried it. That sounds awfully stupid, and it was. I was a young man making a young man's bad mistake.

All athletes fear failure. But some become so obsessed with this ever-present fear that they can find relief only in drugs.

There are also some who fear success. They may suffer from inner conflicts about expressing aggression. Or they may be up against an opponent with such a formidable reputation that they feel defeated before they start. Or they may fear the isolation and envy that sometimes bedevil winners. In any case, escape into drugged oblivion provides an excuse for defeat.

Self-destructiveness and low self-esteem typify many abuser-athletes. For reasons often stemming from family problems and unhappy childhood experiences, they feel secretly unworthy of praise or applause. Turning to drugs is a way of punishing themselves, of erasing themselves— even of toying with suicide.

NONABUSER-ATHLETES

Why do so many other athletes, subject to many of the same stresses, never become dependent on drugs or alcohol? These fortunate individuals form an extremely diverse group. It is difficult to generalize about them, but they tend to share certain characteristics.

They usually were brought up in loving and ego-supporting families. They found positive role models in their parents or some other relative. When they had to be disciplined, it was done firmly but fairly, with love rather than hate. At early stages of development, they were encouraged to develop emotional strength and self-reliance.

These athletes tend to be individuals with a strong sense of self. Rather than following others, they form their own judgments and make their own decisions. They are mature, stable, secure people. They need no chemical boosters to cope with the world around them. At those times when they may occasionally indulge, they remain in control.

Sports psychologists Bruce Ogilvie and Thomas A. Tutko have developed a personality test they call the Athletic Motivation Inventory. It measures eleven traits common to most athletes. After testing thousands of athletes, they have worked out a profile of those who succeed in competition while avoiding drug involvement.

These athletes have a fierce need for achievement, but the goals they set for themselves are realistic. They tend to be orderly, disciplined people. They respect authority, yet have strong and at times even dominant personalities. They are secure enough to trust others and to win the trust of others in return. While they score above the average in aggressiveness, they also rate high in self-control.

In his book-length study of the psychology of athletes, Richard Alderman found the successful ones "outgoing and socially confident . . . warm, good-natured, easygoing, ready to cooperate, attentive to people." Such men have high self-esteem. They "can take rough handling, [are] not easily upset about losing, playing badly, or being spoken to harshly; can accept strong criticism without being hurt." Perhaps most significantly, these are the kinds of competitors who "work harder when the odds seem to be against them."

Nonabuser-athletes are, in short, the opposites in almost every way of the easily misled personalities found among drug and alcohol addicts.

3
ATHLETES UNDER STRESS

Why do so many athletes abuse drugs or alcohol? There are two schools of thought about this. One simply blames the athletes. The other believes the problem is more complicated than that.

Art Rust, Jr., is a popular New York sports commentator. In a recent television interview, he was asked about the causes of athletes' drug abuse. They have the money, Rust said, and they enjoy it— and that's all there is to it:

> I don't buy this idea you hear so much about, that they do it because they're under such awful pressure. They try it, they like it, and they just go on doing it. Using drugs is a way of being part of the "in" group.

Rust's view is shared by many inside and outside of sports. Notable among the sports figures is David J. Stern, National Basketball Association commissioner. Stern told the author that the stresses and strains of sports competition were not so grueling as to drive athletes to drugs or alcohol. "Sure, the players do come under a lot of pressure," Stern said, "but no more than lots of other people in high-tension jobs." He is convinced that athletes actually drink or abuse drugs less than others.

Stern blames the media for the widespread public impression that a high percentage of athletes are into the drug scene. "Nobody hears about it when some ordinary Joe gets high and does something crazy,'' said Stern. ''Let a top athlete do it, and it makes headlines.''

But what kinds of stress do athletes really face? How do the pressures of the sports life compare to the daily wear and tear of ordinary existence?

STARTING YOUNG

The competitive pressures start early in life.

At basketball games featuring top-notch elementary school teams, it is common to find high school coaches scouting talented players. ''Kids are playing rigorous schedules in sixth grade,'' UCLA basketball coach Walt Hazard recently told the *New York Times*. ''By eighth, they're being recruited by high schools. You have newsletters, recruiting reports, scouting services. . . .''

In hockey, it is permissible for high school juniors to be recruited into the professional minor leagues. The result is that youngsters start competing in earnest as early as the fourth grade.

The father of one young football star recalled that by the middle of the boy's eighth-grade season, twelve Catholic high schools were in hot pursuit:

Oh God, they all came after him. Picking him up after school, taking him out for steak dinners, inviting him to basketball games. . . . You're not allowed to give financial aid, but some schools offer to pay tuition. . . .

An estimated 866,000 children twelve years old or younger regularly play some form of organized baseball. About

347,000 play football, 250,000 play basketball, and 36,000 play hockey.

Notre Dame basketball coach Digger Phelps is one of those who have expressed concern about the pressures on children in sports. Phelps says these can result in

> creating a monster, a prima donna, a kid who thinks he's a superstar, who believes the world revolves around him and around sports. I think Little League baseball, for instance, has done much to destroy the proper athletic concepts for young children. There's too much emphasis on winning, on being a star.

Ed Kranepool was a New York Mets star for seventeen years. He has never quite gotten over the contrast between the joyous experience of sandlot baseball games during his childhood, and his more regimented Little League experience. Adults, he says, had nothing to do with the sandlot games. It was just "disorganized fun . . . what sports for little kids should be."

At the age of 10, Kranepool got into the Little Leagues. For him, the adults had too much to say about how the kids played. It was all too overorganized. Much of the joy was gone.

Larry Fox, sports editor of the *New York Daily News,* describes what he calls the "Little League syndrome" as "throwing 8-year-old kids into a must-win situation. That is what leads to drugs in sports."

PAMPERED ATHLETES

A youngster's whole way of life can change as soon as he is discovered to have superior athletic ability. He begins to receive special treatment from parents, teachers, coaches, counselors, friends.

"The elite athletes," says sports psychologist Bruce Ogilvie, "are provided with an unreal world. They're overprotected and pampered. Their lives are so structured that they're cheated out of maturity."

Former New York Jets All-Pro back George Sauer experienced the coddling in ways remembered by hundreds of other players. "You were never given a chance," he says,

> to become responsible or self-disciplined. Even in the pros you are told when to go to bed, when to turn your light off, when to wake up, when to eat and what to eat. You even have to live and eat together like . . . boys in camp. The bad thing about football is that it keeps you in an adolescent stage. . . .

An incident at the University of Arizona back in the early 1970s shows how extreme this overprotection can get. Two top football players admitted to a series of major thefts. They said many of their teammates had helped. The authorities hushed up the whole affair, and no charges were ever filed.

The pampering of athletes gave rise to a landmark lawsuit in 1986. Jan Kemp, an English instructor at the University of Georgia, sued the university. She claimed that she had been demoted and then fired because she had spoken out against favoritism for athletes.

As one example, Kemp cited the case of nine football players who failed her remedial English course. University officials changed their grades to passing so that they could play in an upcoming Sugar Bowl game.

When Kemp protested, she was demoted. She then filed a lawsuit and was dismissed. She filed another lawsuit.

When the case came to trial, the university argued that Kemp had been dismissed because she was disruptive and had not conducted scholarly research. Football coach Vince Dooley testified that enforcing normal grading standards for athletes would "disarm" Georgia's team. The university president asserted that top athletes had special value because they brought the institution millions of dollars in box-office receipts. They therefore deserved special consideration.

The federal jury found the university's actions illegal. It awarded Kemp $2.5 million for lost wages, mental anguish, and punitive damages. This stunning verdict put America's colleges on notice that they had better reconsider their academic standards for athletes.

Sheltered from unpleasant realities for most of their lives, many athletes are not equipped to offer much resistance when illicit pleasures are offered to them. They develop what Pennsylvania Hospital senior psychiatrist Silas L. Warner calls "a sense of entitlement to the best things in life." They begin to believe their own press clippings and feel that they deserve any form of pleasure they can find.

The loneliness brought on by constant travel compounds the problem. When an athlete is alone, says Dr. Warner,

> it is up to him to provide a sense of self-esteem. Many people do not have the inner resources to give themselves such self-esteem. Small wonder, then, that in a lonely hotel room, waiting for something to happen, he dares to try

cocaine. It wipes out instantly any insecurities or doubts he might have harbored. . . .

Dr. Robert O. Voy, director of sports medicine for the U.S. Olympic Committee, expressed a similar view in a letter to the author. Athletes "have too much unused time on their hands," Voy wrote. They "need to escape from public exposure and that means idle time behind closed doors, usually alone." The result is deadly boredom, the "precipitating factor" that leads to drug involvement.

Dr. Arnold M. Washton runs a New Jersey telephone helpline for cocaine abusers. His experience with athletes has convinced him that they live "an extended adolescence, [with] every need taken care of by other personnel." The result is that they "become prime targets for cocaine." Dealers are waiting at the end of every game, eager "to shove it in front of players' noses."

"There are stars and superstars on every team," says Gene Upshaw, executive director of the National Football League Players Association, "who are doing drugs, and the team and the coaches protect them because they are who they are."

WOUNDED MINDS
UCLA psychologist Bryant E. Cratty has studied athletes at all levels. He reports a survey of Little Leaguers indicating that about one-third of the young players showed signs of serious emotional stress stemming from their sports involvement. Their problems ranged from difficulty in eating to unrest at night.

Among high school athletes, Cratty found that one or two members of any typical football team of forty to sixty players were on the verge of a nervous breakdown during a season. At least twelve to fifteen others could benefit from some kind of psychological counseling.

The situation among the pros was equally troubling. On any forty-man team, from five to seven players were likely to evidence symptoms of stomach ulcers during a single season. From a third to a half of the other players showed signs of emotional disturbance, some of them major.

A Philadelphia physician studied nearly three hundred college and professional football players. He found that more than 25 percent were unknowing victims of hypertension (high blood pressure). That is twice the rate of the general population. The disease often stems from long-continued mental stress. If untreated, it can lead to serious heart problems.

Even more shocking is the fact that the physical and mental ordeal that football players go through leaves them with an average life expectancy of only 57. They can look forward to fourteen fewer years of life than the ordinary male citizen.

Most athletes are aware of these gloomy statistics. Understandably, they tend to avoid thinking about them, and some seek artificial means—drugs and alcohol—of blotting out these truths.

Donald M. Fehr, head of the major-league baseball players' union, explained his theory about the sources of stress. Fehr believes that the constant pressure to win causes some of the tension, but "nobody wins all the time." The most severe stress arises from the players' compulsion to perform flawlessly at all times:

> Professional baseball is the ultimate "what-have-you-done-for-me-lately" business. Somebody is always coming up who is younger, who is smarter, who is cheaper for the club to hire, who has better training, who is better coordinated and a little faster. His goal in life is to take your job.

The players are keenly aware, too, that most major-league careers are short. Players who make it through all the prior levels of competition to the majors last an average of four years.

Fehr pointed to the large numbers of young hopefuls coming out of the colleges and junior colleges, and even the high schools, who get into the minor leagues. They keep trying for the majors. Most never make it. Then they suddenly discover that they're pushing 30, that they have no other skills or training or professional education, that they're six or seven years behind their peers in terms of career progress. They've never made any real money, and they don't have any—and they have to start over. "That," said Fehr, "is enormous pressure."

Columnist Leonard Koppett has befriended and studied athletes over the course of many years. Noting their tendency to "extreme nervous tension," he points out that it is "shared by all professional performers."

Such tension is inevitable, Koppett says, in people who "live high-intensity lives in brief and hazardous careers." Their professions "require constant traveling and considerable loneliness. . . ." Such people will inevitably "produce among their number a certain proportion of people who seek relief in drugs."

The intensity of athletic competition itself produces feelings that athletes enjoy. Win or lose, they come off the playing field or leave the gym very aroused, their adrenaline flowing. They want to maintain that high. Alcohol and drugs let them hold on to it—at least for a while.

When the average individual does something wrong, it rarely draws the attention of more than a few people. But the football player who drops a pass, the baseball player who strikes out or commits an error, the basketball player who keeps missing layups—they must all bear the loud and often brutal derision of thousands.

Similarly, most people with drug or drinking problems affect the lives of only a few other individuals. They can seek help quietly and confidentially. But athletes' problems are well publicized, with sensational rumors about them often given the biggest headlines.

During his unmatched seventeen-year career as the NBA's most durable star, Kareem Abdul-Jabbar has seen how the pressure cooker of professional sports works on athletes' weaknesses:

> Players are under pressure to perform by management, the fans, their peers, themselves. Relaxation is a necessity, and drugs help that right along. Some guys drink; that's just as dangerous. . . . Others get high.

But Kareem feels that most athletes can stand the strain without cracking. They "have developed the ability to withstand and even channel the pressure to their benefit, the same way they developed their inside moves.''

For younger athletes, the pressure can be more damaging. ''Athletic success,'' says psychologist Cratty, ''may be the 'glue' which is holding a youngster together.'' It becomes especially important in cases where the athlete's family is not stable, or not supportive.

When such a youth encounters failure on the field, his entire personality may disintegrate. ''The youngster may be derided daily by his coach, periodically by the press, and may even be rejected by members of his family, if the team is not having a successful season.''

The result may be ''despair . . . inappropriate aggression and antisocial behaviors.'' These behaviors can and often do include a turn toward drugs. In some cases they end in suicide.

THE SHAME OF THE COLLEGES

Colleges and universities are supposed to be educational institutions first and foremost. Their other activities, including sports, are supposed to be subordinate to education. The trouble is that sports have become such an important source of revenue and prestige to some colleges that they get top priority.

A public confession made recently by the president of the University of Southern California was a notable example. He signed a report acknowledging that, over a ten-year period, USC had admitted no fewer than 330 athletes who did not meet the school's minimum academic requirements.

USC also had to forfeit the NCAA track championship, when it was revealed that a star sprinter had been admitted on the basis of credits allegedly earned—all at the same time—at four widely separated junior colleges.

One athlete, from Englewood High School in Chicago, was given a decidedly special entrance exam at Indiana State. All that was asked of him was that he name the twelve months of the year. Though he could name only ten, he passed.

Alan Beals was for seven years the University of Tennessee's academic counselor for athletes. He resigned in June 1984 as a protest against the school's recruiting policies. "Frankly," Beals said, "they've recruited some guys I'm not sure I can keep in school."

What happens to ill-prepared students after their sports skills get them into college? There have been some heart-wrenching cases.

Billy Don Jackson had been recruited to play football for the University of California at Los Angeles. By his junior year, he seemed certain to make All-American and be drafted by the pros.

Then some of his teammates discovered that Jackson was barely able to read. They began to mock him, calling him "Billy Dum-Dum." Always shy and sensitive, Jackson became extremely withdrawn. He had tried cocaine for fun; now he became a serious addict.

Jackson had a fight with his drug dealer. When it ended, the dealer was dead. Jackson went to jail. It was only there that he finally began to learn to read and write.

Jackson's case is not exceptional. There are colleges in every part of the country where fewer than 10 percent of athletes on scholarships ever graduate. And there are others where athletes' academic progress is carefully monitored, where support by counselors and tutors is made available, and where three-quarters or more of scholarship athletes graduate.

Even athletes who arrive at college with sound academic training and ability have difficulty keeping up. They spend four hours or more per day practicing. They miss classes for road trips. They experience mental stress and physical pain that most students never encounter.

Athletes tend to be dreamers. The dream that sustains those who move through school and college without paying much attention to their studies is the tantalizing fantasy of a rich pro contract. For the vast majority, it turns out to be an empty dream.

Consider the odds in basketball and football. About 700,000 boys play high school basketball. The number in football is about a million. By the time they reach the college varsity level, those figures have been slashed to 15,000 in basketball and 41,000 in football.

Some 4,000 basketball players stay in college to the end. Of these, only 200 get drafted by NBA teams. A mere 50 of the draftees actually make the teams. And after all the years of single-minded dedication and sacrifice, the average pro career lasts a brief 3.4 seasons.

The annual NFL draft calls up 320 college football players. A little fewer than half get pro contracts. They last an average of 4.2 seasons.

"For every youth lifted out of a coal-mining town or taken from a ghetto by an athletic scholarship," says University of California sociologist Harry Edwards, "there are hundreds of other lower-class youths who have wasted their lives futilely preparing to be a sports star.''

What goes on in the minds and emotions of young men facing these grim realities? Former New York Knicks forward Bill Bradley, now a U.S. senator, tells what it is like:

> There is terror behind the dream of being a professional ballplayer. . . . When the playing is over, one can sense that one's youth has been spent playing a game, and now both the youth and the game are gone. . . . Now the athlete must face a world where [immaturity] can no longer be overlooked because of athletic performance. By age 35 any potential for developing skills outside of [sports] is slim. . . . For the athlete who reaches 35, something in him dies. . . .

Most athletes find practical, sensible ways to cope with these special problems of the sports life. But others go on trying to build their lives on dreams. And that is where drugs and booze come in. They soften unpleasant facts; they make a tough life livable; for a little while, they make dreams seem real.

4

THE PERSISTENT EVIL: RACISM

A powerful force has been at work in American sports for many decades. Its name is racism, and it is often ignored by those who do not suffer under its influence.

Black, Hispanic, and other minority athletes experience all the mental, emotional, and physical stresses that white athletes feel. But they also bear a heavy extra burden, in the persistence of racial prejudice and discrimination. Though there has been impressive progress against it in recent years, racism still pervades sports as profoundly as it affects other aspects of American life.

THE REVOLUTION IN RACE RELATIONS

As a rookie in 1957, I was the only black player on the Boston Celtics, and I was excluded from almost everything except practice and the games. Exactly twenty years later I was coach and general manager of the Seattle Supersonics, which had only two white players on the team—and they were excluded from everything but practice and the games. . . . I told the blacks how unfair this was, and they made a token effort to change. . . . In basketball, it took only twenty years to go from the outhouse to the in-crowd.
—Bill Russell, Second Wind, *1979*

No other aspect of sports has changed more dramatically than the treatment of black athletes. Only forty years ago, most big-time sports were closed to blacks. The vast majority of high schools and colleges fielded lily-white teams. This was hardly surprising, since the teams were drawn from all-white student bodies. The professional teams were equally "pure." Even the seating arrangements for the fans at many major athletic events were segregated.

Practically the only place black athletes could be seen in team sports was in games matching all-black schools and colleges, or in baseball's Negro leagues. The white majority of the general public ignored these.

Black athletes found two sports more accessible: boxing and track. Ever since 1908, when Jack Johnson became the first black to win the world heavyweight title, an impressive number of black fighters had triumphed over racial prejudice and discrimination—and their opponents—to capture championships. Today blacks dominate the heavier weight divisions and also hold some of the lighter weight titles.

In track, a few outstanding black runners had achieved distinction. A special inspiration to generations of aspiring blacks was Jesse Owens, who achieved the then unprecedented feat of winning four gold medals at the 1936 Olympics. Black Americans in recent years have been especially successful at the shorter distances, while black Africans have competed strongly in longer runs.

The historic change in major team sports began soon after World War II. The breakthrough year was 1947, when Jackie Robinson broke the color barrier in major-league baseball. The following year, a black was signed to play pro football. Then, in 1950, two black players got contracts with National Basketball Association teams. The door had started to open, and talented black athletes were soon flooding through it.

The numbers reflect the scope of the transformation. Pro basketball today has the highest proportion of black players, 74 percent. In pro football, more than 55 percent of the players are black. For complicated reasons, the figure in major-league baseball is lower, though still substantial: nearly 20 percent. These figures must be measured against the fact that blacks make up only 12 percent of the U.S. population.

As for college sports, of the 90,000 athletes who participate in football, baseball, and basketball, about half are black. Yet black students form a bare 1.5 percent of the total college population.

Blacks have not only broken through—they actually dominate the major sports in virtually every performance category. They produce a disproportionate number of baseball's batting and fielding and stolen-base champions, basketball's top scorers and rebounders and blockers, football's record-setting pass receivers and running backs.

Sports such as tennis, golf, and swimming resisted integration longer. But blacks are now competing successfully in these fields, too, and have won championships in all of them. Tennis stars Arthur Ashe and Althea Gibson and golf master Calvin Peete are notable among those who have led the way.

It was not until 1983 that a black swimmer first competed as a member of a U.S. team in an international meet. That year, Chris Silva won a silver medal at the World University Games. He was already the holder of the American record for the 400-yard freestyle.

Still another barrier fell in February 1986, when Debi Thomas became the first black skater to win the U.S. Figure

Skating championship. Her four-minute freeskating program included a spectacular series of five triple-jumps.

Clearly, the change has been nothing short of revolutionary. "Sport in America in the 1980s," says columnist Leonard Koppett, "has come further toward true integration with less ongoing turmoil than, let us say, central-city school systems or the nationwide job market. . . ."

But have prejudice and discrimination been driven out of sports? The painful but inescapable answer is that they have not.

BLACK ADDICTS, WHITE ADDICTS

Does the extra burden of racism cause black athletes to abuse drugs and alcohol more than their white teammates? Large segments of the public have long been convinced that this is so. No study has yet been done that specifically compares drug and alcohol addiction rates for white and black athletes. But there are statistics for addicts of both races drawn from the general population.

Dr. Lawrence Kirstein is clinical director of Regent Hospital in New York City, one of the nation's leading drug treatment centers. His studies of the cocaine market indicated that slightly more than 85 percent of its customers are white.

Another recent survey, focusing on drug users admitted to federally funded drug treatment programs, showed that twice as many white males were admitted as blacks. Patients in treatment units were about 15 percent black, a figure just slightly above the proportion of blacks in the U.S. population. Studies comparing alcoholism rates among black and white males showed no significant differences.

The athletes blame the media for the widespread notion that black athletes drink more, and take drugs more, than whites. Black athletes with drinking or drug problems get more negative publicity than white athletes, they contend. As one example, they point to the almost total lack of publicity given to the drinking and drug habits of the all-white teams in the National Hockey League.

It contradicts common sense to assume that so many black athletes could perform at such superior levels if they were more prone to drug abuse than their white teammates. The evidence that is available indicates only that athletes of both races have gotten deeply involved in the drug scene. The balance between black and white abusers of drugs and alcohol is doubtless a constantly shifting one.

THE THORNY BARRIERS

Once the black athlete has made it into high-level competition, he faces new forms of discrimination. He is likely to have a hard time getting assigned to a leadership or decision-making position on the field. There are, for instance, few black quarterbacks on the major college teams, and almost none in the pros. Blacks are concentrated in the most injury-prone positions. Nearly 90 percent of the running backs are black, and nearly 80 percent of the wide receivers.

In baseball, some black players feel that the managers resist placing them in key infield positions, especially pitcher and catcher. In the mid-1980s, there was not a single black catcher in the major leagues, and catchers, with their view of the entire field, often play an important part in determining team strategy. As for pitchers, fewer than 7 percent were black.

An enlightening view of the background to this problem was provided to the author during a lengthy interview with former Denver Broncos defensive back Ernie Parker. He is now a drug counselor at the Center for the Study of Sports in Society, at Boston's Northeastern University.

Parker served at one time as a "Pop Warner" football coach in Hampton, Virginia. There, the young teams were integrated, with roughly equal proportions of black and white players. Parker noted that the white parents— especially the fathers, of course—showed up in large numbers at practices and games. Very few black fathers ever came. Parker explained that many more of the black kids came from fatherless homes than the white kids. Even where black fathers were present in the home, they often worked two jobs and could not attend practice sessions.

This difference became crucially important when the time came to assign the kids to positions. Some of the white fathers pressured the coaches to give their sons a shot at the choice positions, such as quarterback or linebacker. Even when the fathers remained passive on the sidelines, the coaches were influenced by their presence.

Parker noted that the black youngsters seemed resigned to the situation. With no one to back them up, they didn't even try for the leadership slots.

Multiplied many times in settings throughout the country, patterns of behavior like this one foreshadow the racial setup at schools, colleges, and in the pros. A difference between the races that originates in social, economic, and cultural factors becomes a source of discrimination in sports.

Basketball's five-man teams are too small to allow for keeping black players out of any position. But nevertheless, a kind of racial quota system operates in basketball (it is less apparent in other sports).

It stems from the fact that basketball audiences are predominantly white, and many white fans dislike watching all-black teams. The result is that the coaches feel pressured to field at least one and usually more white players, even if it means keeping better black ones on the bench.

Some years ago the New York Knicks dared to experiment with an all-black eleven-man squad. The fans' protests were immediate, loud, and insistent. They taunted the team as "the New York 'Niggerbockers.' " The experiment was soon abandoned.

Basketball Hall of Famer Bill Russell commented sardonically on this situation nearly twenty years ago: "The practice is to put two black athletes in the basketball game at home, put three in on the road, put four in when you're losing, and put five in during the playoffs." This unwritten rule may have been eased somewhat in the years since then, but it still exercises a hidden influence.

Black basketball players also have to perform better than whites in order to stay on the teams. White players whose scoring records are significantly lower than blacks' will be drafted and kept on the teams, while blacks with better averages may not even get drafted. The average career scoring record for whites in the NBA is 9.3. The black average is 11.1.

For obvious reasons, sports business offices keep a close watch on their teams' TV ratings and attendance. Experience has shown that basketball teams that are largely black must win at least 70 percent of their games to hold on to their audiences. Predominantly white teams can do worse without suffering serious losses in popularity.

In baseball, there is reason to believe that the already relatively low percentage of blacks will soon decline even further. Management has been cutting back sharply on the minor-league system, which once trained and developed most of the major-league players. There were 59 minor-league teams in 1949; there are only about 17 today. The major-league teams have no alternative but to do more of their recruiting from the colleges, where there are far fewer black candidates for baseball jobs. In 1971, blacks made up 29 percent of the players in both leagues. That percentage has already slipped below 20 and seems certain to fall further.

WHERE ARE THE BLACK COACHES?

"It's pretty hard to excuse the fact," says veteran wide receiver Ahmad Rashad, "that, in [pro football] where over 50 percent of the players are black, there are no black head coaches. . . ." This fact stands out all the more starkly when you consider that there has been a turnover of ninety-one head coaches on the NFL's 28 teams since 1975.

Eddie Robinson, football coach at small, rural, all-black Grambling College, became the winningest coach in the history of college football in October 1985. That was when he won his 324th victory, surpassing even the legendary

Paul "Bear" Bryant of the mighty University of Alabama. Nearly two hundred of the players Robinson trained have been drafted by the NFL—another record unmatched by any other college coach.

Yet black coach Robinson has never been offered a job as head coach by any major college or pro team. "I would at least like the opportunity to turn down a job," he says. "Every white coach in the country with my tenure has had that chance."

In all fairness, the chances for a black to be appointed to a top coaching job in pro football are improving. By the 1985–1986 season, the number of black assistant coaches had risen to thirty-four, far above the number only a few years earlier.

Tony Dungy, black defensive coordinator for the Pittsburgh Steelers, discussed the problem with *New York Times* sports columnist Dave Anderson:

> Most of the NFL owners are old school, they hire guys they're familiar with. . . . But some day an owner is going to be comfortable with a black guy he interviews. That's when it's going to happen. . . .

Pro basketball, the "blackest" of the major sports, has had a total of twelve black head coaches over the past twenty years. There have been as many as three at one time (in the 1982–1983 season). Considering that there are twenty-three coaching spots available, that is not a very high proportion. And the number of black coaches has dropped to two since then.

At the college level, the number of black coaches is only a little higher. In 1985 there were nine black head basketball coaches in the 269 Division I colleges. These are schools with predominantly white student bodies, but the majority of their basketball players are black.

In baseball, in all the years since Jackie Robinson's breakthrough, the twenty-six major-league teams have so far found places for only three black managers. Each held the job for a short period. Of the 123 coaches who assist the managers, thirteen are black.

Discrimination in sports is also obvious in front-office jobs, such as general manager or personnel director. In no major sport has a black been appointed to these positions.

Some observers feel that this circumstance is at least partly due to the fact that black and white players tend to go their separate ways off the field. As is true in American society generally, the two races seldom spend their leisure hours together.

But advancement in sports business offices depends on the same factors as in business everywhere. It is a kind of "buddy system." Management officials tend to promote individuals they know socially, or whom others know and recommend. Until the social barriers between the races break down, blacks' advancement into these privileged ranks will remain difficult.

THE SADDEST FAILURE: ACADEMICS

Nowhere are the patterns of discrimination more obvious than in the academic sphere. Only 6 percent of all college athletic scholarships go to black applicants. More than a quarter of the black high school athletes who qualify for these scholarships have to turn them down because their educational preparation is inadequate. Of blacks able to accept the scholarships, a shocking 65 to 75 percent do not complete the course requirements for graduation. The comparable figure for white athletes is 25 to 35 percent.

Both black and white players are usually guided by coaches or counselors to take easy, worthless courses so that they can concentrate on the sport they have been brought to the school to play. The result is that they have to leave college after four or five years with no degree and no preparation for any kind of meaningful career outside of sports.

Of the black athletes who do graduate, almost two-thirds receive degrees in physical education or some little-respected major created especially for athletes. Only a select few win contracts with pro teams. The vast majority have little in the way of skills or training or knowledge to offer in the career marketplace. "Allowing athletes, black or white, to go unchallenged scholastically," says *Sports Illustrated* writer John Underwood, "is a permission slip to heartbreak."

A variety of excuses is usually cited for the colleges' abysmal record with black athletes. Some sociologists point out that these students often come from socially restricted and economically deprived backgrounds, that their prior education in ghetto schools has been inferior, and that low standards have been set for them throughout their school careers.

UCLA professor of sociology Harry Edwards argues that " 'dumb jocks' are not born, they're systematically created." The remedy, he says, is to raise the academic requirements for all athletes. Educators who resist higher standards for black athletes "underestimate . . . the black athletes' capabilities to rise to the academic challenges. . . ."

Most of the colleges have done little to remedy the athletes' scholastic deficiencies. Joe Paterno of Penn State, twice voted "Football Coach of the Year," bluntly warned the convention of the National Collegiate Athletic Association:

> For fifteen years we have had a race problem. We've raped them. We've told black kids who bounce balls, run around tracks and catch touchdown passes that that is an end unto itself. We've raped them. We can't afford to do it to another generation.

THE UNQUENCHABLE DREAM

For blacks and members of other minority groups, living in a prejudiced society is like walking with heavy weights on their legs. For black athletes in the relentless competition of big-time sports, it is like carrying the opposing team on one's back.

Yet they do it—and they do it amazingly well. And millions of eager black youngsters spend their waking hours preparing for the chance to do it, too. Their dream is to climb out of the ghetto, to beat poverty and unemployment, to make it to those fat salaries and the glory and the fame.

Few will make it. Even fewer realize that prejudice and discrimination await them even at the top.

Some of these youngsters come to sports as no strangers to drugs or drink. They find these easily available throughout the sports world. Whether or not they get hooked depends on many factors; racism is only one of them. But it runs so deep, it hurts so much, it persists so stubbornly, that it demands special understanding.

5

THE GOOD COACH AND THE BAD COACH

Imagine a good coach and a bad coach vying for the heart and mind of an athlete.

The good coach trains the athlete to a peak of physical condition. He teaches the athlete the skills needed for hard-fought victories. He emphasizes good sportsmanship and fair play. He gives the youngster a solid basis on which to go out and win the world's acclaim, its big-money rewards.

At the same time, the good coach warns the athlete against our pleasure-oriented, drug-ridden society. The athlete must not let any of society's false values influence him. He must resist immoral or illegal temptations. He has a special responsibility to stand as a shining example to the youth of the nation.

The bad coach's advice is more complicated—but to far too many athletes, it sounds like more fun.

Win at any cost, the bad coach commands the athlete. Win within the rules if you can, outside them if you have to. Hit hard. Whether the hit is clean or not doesn't matter. Winning is all that matters.

Start winning by the time you're eight or nine. Keep building your athletic reputation through junior and senior high school. Ignore your studies. It will be easy to persuade your teachers to give you passing grades.

When the time comes for you to get into college, someone will find a way to get you an athletic scholarship. There are plenty of colleges and universities that value sports winners over scholars.

During your senior year in high school (maybe even during your junior year), your fine athletic record will draw the college recruiters as honey draws flies. Choose carefully among them.

Which of them offers the biggest under-the-table payoffs, the flashiest cars, the best-looking girls, the highest-paying "jobs" with no work involved? Which will guarantee you the most academic credits for the easiest courses, or even for courses you'll never bother to attend? Which will best improve your chances of making the pros?

Once you've made it into college, concentrate even harder on your sports skills. Don't worry about your academic record; leave that to your coaches and counselors. They'll see to it that you remain eligible to play as long as you're needed.

Keep hitting hard, keep winning, and you'll be a sure bet to reach the top. You'll become a professional. Don't even think about what comes later. Pro sports will make you so rich you won't ever have to worry about money.

Enjoy your sudden wealth *now*. Live high. Ride the fast lane. Use anything that helps you relax.

So what if most pro sports careers last fewer than five years. That's for other guys to worry about. You're in to stay. For you, the money and the cheers and the good times will never stop.

If you get hurt playing, forget it. Stay in the game. If necessary, let the trainer shoot up your injury with novocaine or some other painkiller. You're young, you're strong, you'll heal fast. Nothing can really hurt you for long. Remember, there's always some young hotshot ready and eager to take your place.

Go for that winning edge over your opponents. Take the pep pills, the steroids, the human growth hormones. They may give you that extra hundredth of a second's speed, that intimidating extra inch of muscle, that extra foot-pound of strength, that kill-or-be-killed aggressiveness, that unbeatable stamina.

Dangerous side effects? What do they matter, compared to the rewards of victory?

Of course, no real-life coach would ever give such extreme advice. But this exaggerated example does give a fair sampling of the kinds of tips many athletes get from many coaches. All too often, the bad coach outtalks the good. Athletes are only human, after all. The temptations open to them are often harder to resist than those that may occasionally be offered to the rest of us.

WIN, WIN, WIIINNN!

An old-time sportswriter named Grantland Rice once wrote a little poem that expressed a perhaps corny but sincere notion of sportsmanship. Part of it went like this:

> When the One Great Scorer comes to write against your
>   name—
> He marks—not that you won or lost—but how you played
>   the game.

Today, the idea that playing fair might be more important than winning seems almost quaint. What today's team members hear from some coaches is very different.

Here, for example, is George Allen, longtime coach of the Washington Redskins and one of pro football's winningest coaches: "Only winners are truly alive. Winning is living. Every time you win, you're reborn. When you lose, you die a little."

Then there's the statement often attributed to the late Vince Lombardi, coach of the Green Bay Packers in their Super Bowl years: "Winning isn't everything. It's the *only* thing."

Way back in the 1940s, Brooklyn Dodger manager Leo "The Lip" Durocher used to warn his players: "Nice guys finish last."

James Kehoe, director of athletics at the University of Maryland, gives his players a little introductory speech at the start of every season. It includes the following:

> I don't buy losing. . . . I see nothing commendable or outstanding about finishing anything but first. . . . Whoever you might be in this room, if you don't want to be the best, then you're not going to work for me.

Teams that fail to win have traditionally gotten flayed by their coaches. Some coaches carry the tradition very far. Columbia University football coach Jim Garrett was so infuriated by his team's lopsided loss of a game to Harvard in September 1985 that he called them a bunch of "drug-addicted losers." The university replaced Garrett soon afterward.

Another example of bad coaching occurred recently in Taylor Mill, Kentucky. The juniors and seniors on the Scott High School basketball team charged coach Jim Mitchell with physical and mental abuse. They petitioned the school administration to remove him. Then they walked off the squad. Mitchell was said to have struck players on at least two occasions, and to have ridden team members constantly.

"He runs you down until you hate the game," said senior Barry Curtis, team cocaptain. "He's all the time telling us we're no good. One game this year we beat a pretty good team, and he told us we didn't deserve to win." Mitchell had only a one-year contract. He was allowed to complete it.

Such coaches feel that they cannot leave any doubt about how they want their players to behave on the field. They are under pressure themselves in the constant struggle to get their contracts renewed or to ensure funding for their teams and athletic departments. Ceaselessly and raucously, they hammer away with their demands for flawless performance. The penalties they impose for anything less are swift and severe.

The athletes know only too clearly what to expect. And that knowledge can be too stressful for young minds to bear.

VIOLENCE ON THE RISE

In recent years there has been an alarming increase in sports violence. It is both a cause and a result of drug abuse among athletes.

Violence is a cause, since players facing brutality on the field tend to rely on drugs as a way of coping with it. And it is a result, because players steeped in drugs are capable of violent behavior they might otherwise avoid.

The violence takes many forms:

—On one side of the field, the ball is called dead as a crunching tackle halts forward movement on the play. On the other side is Pittsburgh wide receiver Lynn Swann, one of pro football's smaller and slimmer players, who has been distant from the action. Swann starts back up the field. Suddenly he is clobbered to the ground by a vicious forearm thrown at the back of his head by Oakland safety man George Atkinson. The resulting concussion keeps Swann out of action for weeks.

—Goal tender Billy Smith of the Islanders drops to the ice, hit in the throat by the puck after a Canuck slap shot. After several minutes, he feels able to continue. In the second period, Smith and Canuck "Tiger" Williams get into a shoving match close to Smith's goal. Williams knocks Smith down, pulls off the goalie's helmet, and starts punching.

"Everyone knows I was hurt," Smith says later. He claims Williams first threw an elbow at his injured throat and then "all of a sudden I feel his hands around my throat. That's pretty tacky."

—During a recent Chicago Bears–Green Bay Packers game, Bears quarterback Jim McMahon throws a pass and is watching the ball hurtle toward the receiver. Three seconds have gone by when Packers nose tackle Charles Martin grabs McMahon and slams him down on his neck and shoulder. Martin is thrown out of the game and suspended for two additional games, but appeals the suspensions.

—About eight feet out from the basket, Lakers center Kareem Abdul-Jabbar is jockeying for position inside the lane. The opposing guard smashes an elbow into his ribs. The referee catches the illicit act out of the corner of an eye, but decides to let it go this time.

After all, Kareem is such a formidable player that he'd be almost impossible to stop if the other team weren't allowed a little extra leeway. This happens so often that Kareem hardly bothers to protest anymore.

Competitors who brutalize their opponents are not always acting on their own. Coaches and managers have trained and encouraged them to do it from their earliest days in sports. Team members' jobs sometimes depend on how violent they can be. NFL defensive star Scott Perry describes the cult of violence:

> Players are taught to run through their opponent's body, to accelerate on impact and knock 'em into next week. There is absurdity in defending the adage "I didn't really want to hurt him" when, if you knock your opponent out of the game, you've performed your job to the maximum. How do you knock somebody out of a game without hurting him?

Roger Staubach, longtime quarterback for the Dallas Cowboys, is one of those who sees a link between much of today's violence and the rise of drug abuse. He told a "60 Minutes" TV interviewer, "I used to stare across the line of scrimmage and see a linebacker whose eyes weren't both going the same way, and there was a little frothing. . . ." Staubach knew what to expect from a player in that hopped-up condition: out-of-control violence.

Staubach placed the blame on "that sinister element [that] hovers around these players [who] sometimes aren't as mature as they should be." The "sinister element" is, of course, the drug dealers.

Players found to be under the influence of drugs when they injure others by illegal violence may soon find themselves held legally liable for the injuries. NFL commissioner Pete Rozelle is one of those who has urged such policies, "for the health and welfare of the players—those taking drugs and those injured by those taking drugs."

The severity of many recent injuries has prompted one insurance firm, State Mutual Life Assurance Co. of America, to stop issuing new policies to players or teams for disabling injuries. Ted Dipple, president of American Sports Underwriters, told reporters that the extreme violence caused by drugs and steroid abuse was the main reason for the insurers' decision.

Football fans, too, blame drug abuse for a high proportion of violence and injuries. In a recent *New York Times*/CBS Sports poll, only "dirty play" was rated a bigger cause of injuries than drugs. And in many people's minds, dirty play and drugs were clearly linked.

Considering the kind of athletic training some youngsters get these days, their tendency to violence when they get older should surprise no one. A startling example is reproduced in sportswriter John Underwood's recent book, *Death of an American Game*. These were the instructions handed to an 8-year-old Little League football player by his coach:

Punish the tackler! Put fear in his eyes! Bruise his body!
Break his spirit! Bust his butt! Make him pay a price for
tackling you!
    Be hostile! Be angry! Be violent! Be mean! Be aggressive!
Be physical!

To demonstrate the vicious spirit that can be produced
by that kind of coaching, Underwood quotes a letter from
an Oklahoma high school football player. The teenager
boasted that any time he has to throw an illegal block, or
"throw a forearm to [my opponent's] windpipe, I'm going
to do just that." When he tackles a runner, he pledged that
he would "put my face mask into his numbers so hard that
I hope he never gets up. Someday I hope to teach the way
I play. Stick him before he sticks you."
    Clearly, drastic measures are necessary to reduce the vi-
olence that pervades team sports today. Until that happens,
athletes facing the grim prospect of combat on the field are
likely to go right on looking for whatever forms of psychic
relief they can find.

6
PLAYING WITH PAIN

Stepped-up violence inevitably produces an ever-mounting toll of injuries. But when a team desperately needs a player who is hurt, a whole array of drugs is available to keep the athlete on the field.

THE CASUALTY COUNT

Counting up the wounded in today's sports produces numbers so high they seem more fitted to a war than to games supposedly played for fun and profit.

An estimated 12 million Americans under 18 have suffered permanent disabilities from sports injuries. Some of these are not serious, but others are crippling.

Football's injury count is the highest. Over 40,000 players require surgery every year. The annual toll of high school players injured is fully a million. The death toll was at one time close to fifty. Fortunately, the number of football players killed has dropped substantially in the 1980s, to about eight per year.

The only other bright spots are a 75 percent decline in the number of disabling spinal injuries among high school and college players, and a 22 percent drop in head injuries. These welcome reductions are the result of rule changes that outlaw "spearing" and other head-first tackling methods.

Until recently, about ninety youngsters a year endured broken necks playing football. A third of these suffered the tragedy of quadriplegia (paralysis from the neck down).

With the new rules, the number of paralyzed players dropped to five in 1984.

One football season, a single Indiana high school reported four broken backs, four broken legs, and an uncounted number of torn ligaments and cartilage. Fifteen lettermen had to have major surgery. And the season was only half over.

At over nine hundred colleges, 70,000 football players get hurt in an average year. The rate among the NFL's professionals is 100 percent, meaning that as many injuries are recorded each year as there are players.

In theory at least, basketball is not supposed to be as violent a body-contact sport as football or hockey. But basketball injuries are mounting steeply. Consider just one team, the Knicks. Between September 5, 1984, and November 3, 1985, its players suffered a total of twenty-four major injuries. Knick players missed 325 games during the 1984–1985 season. Several involved key men, who were out for months or even the entire season.

Dr. Norman Scott, the Knicks' physician, blames the increased injuries on recent changes in the way basketball is played:

The pace of the game has quickened. More emphasis has been placed on running and jumping, and those are factors which make players more vulnerable to injury. . . . With the advent of the two-team system, more players are involved in more stressful minutes. Pressure defenses have added to the fatigue factor. . . .

Dr. Scott believes the number of injuries could be reduced "if we could eliminate back-to-back games and three and four games a week." But he knows that is unrealistic. The NBA schedule requires the teams to "crowd an 82-game schedule into a limited number of days."

THE WALKING WOUNDED

Professional athletes . . . are well tuned to the proposition that they might need help to face extreme pain, or to mask it. Team physicians . . . stuff them with codeine, drug their knees with Xylocain, shoot their inflamed joints with cortisone. Playing hurt, or in pain, is a badge of courage in football. . . .
—*John Underwood,* The Death of an American Game, *1979*

In January 1986, the football Giants were facing a tough playoff game against the nearly unbeaten Chicago Bears. Three of the Giants' defensive backs had suffered leg injuries in a game the previous week. All were grimly determined to play. Said Elvis Patterson: "I wouldn't sit out this one for the world. Hurtin' doesn't matter now." Ted Watts chimed in: "I'm sore as hell, but nothing's going to keep me out."

New York Jets nose tackle Joe Klecko is another of those whose love of the game drives him to play hurt. "The body may not be hitting on all cylinders," he told a *Newsday* reporter, "but you tape it together and keep rolling if you want to keep collecting that hefty paycheck."

Klecko played several games during the 1982 season with an injured right knee. He was in great pain during a game against the New England Patriots, but resisted the suggestion that he sit out the rest of the game. During one especially violent play, the patella tendon in his kneecap ruptured. This most dangerous of all knee injuries would have ended a less determined player's career. Klecko went through many months of grueling rehabilitation to become once again the terror of opposing quarterbacks.

Brent Ziegler may not be so lucky. He had signed himself out of Syracuse University to join the USFL's New Jersey Generals as a rookie fullback. Ziegler had a foot injury that could have kept him out of an exhibition game against Tampa Bay. But he was eager to show the coaches that he could play with pain. Ziegler came out of the game with a knee so badly shattered that there was little hope he'd ever play again.

Adding insult to injury, the Generals then released him. The team's insurance paid his medical expenses, but as a rookie he received no further salary. There was no way he could be in shape to earn any sort of independent living for at least a year.

"I thought football was my way to money and success," says Ziegler, "but when God closes the door He opens a window, and I just got to find that window. . . ."

Bob Chandler played in the NFL (Buffalo and Cleveland) for twelve seasons. He suffered nine operations, broke a hand, cracked a vertebra, lost his spleen, had a collapsed lung, and tore his knee ligaments.

A *USA Today* reporter asked Chandler why he kept at it.

The "biggest pressure," said Chandler, was that "you know someone is going to come in and take your job." He played soon after his spleen surgery, and again "on a broken foot that I would shoot with Xylocain, but those were decisions I made."

At a recent reunion of Hall of Fame members, former Philadelphia Eagles running back Steve Van Buren recalled similar experiences. He played one season with four broken ribs, a broken toe, and a sprained ankle:

> I used to take twelve shots of Novocain a game. You'd get used to the needles. The only time it bothered me was when the doc hit the bone. [The needles would] break when they hit the bone.

Bill Walton is universally rated as one of the greatest all-around basketball players. In the late 1970s, when he played center and team leader for the Portland Trail Blazers, he hurt his foot. With his team about to enter the playoffs, Walton reluctantly took shots for it. He got no further than the second playoff game, when he broke the injured foot. That was the end of the season for him, and the end of the team's playoff hopes as well. For the rest of his NBA career, Walton seldom played without pain.

In his book about sports violence, *Seasons of Shame,* Robert Yeager gives an example that shows how powerful some of the painkilling drugs can be. He notes the case of basketball player Bobby Gross, who "was so numbed by [Xylocain] that only by hearing the cracking bone could he tell when he broke his own leg."

None of these cases surprises Dr. Joseph D. Godfrey, team physician for the Buffalo Bills. Pregame shots of pain-killers, Godfrey told *Physician and Sportsmedicine* magazine, "virtually ensure that players will hurt themselves more seriously. You don't give aspirin and then tell a man to go bang his head."

The choices of whether to play hurt, and whether to let injuries be shot up with drugs, are not always up to the player. Neil D. Isaacs has learned this lesson from some of his students. Isaacs, a professor of English at the University of Maryland, teaches a course in the culture of sports. Athletes taking the course are required to keep a journal, in which they record their thoughts and feelings. One football player was brutally honest:

> If a player is hurt the [coach] tells Doc to shoot him up and let him play—they worry about injury after we win or lose. The one really big gripe I have is that if you are hurt and you cannot help the program any more, the coaching staff will do anything in their power to get you to quit so they can give your scholarship to someone else.

Another player wrote, "I have seen too many players inserted back into the lineup without proper time to heal their various wounds and injuries." And another: "A lot of doctors will go against their will if the coach says he wants a certain player ready by game day. The doctor is then under pressure, so he will shoot [the player] up if he has to."

Pressured situations like these have occasionally led to tragedy. Such was the case for Detroit Lions tight end Charlie Sanders. A brilliant pass receiver, he had been voted into the Pro Bowl seven times. Then he hurt his knee. The team doctors treated the knee by wiring it, shooting electrical charges through it, and wrapping it heavily.

Sanders complained of terrible pain. The coaches hinted to the press that he was dogging it. He kept playing. Finally the knee was reexamined through a then-new process called arthroscopy. The bone was discovered to be completely rotted out. Sanders' career was over.

On rare occasions, an athlete wins compensation after his health and career have been damaged by injections he was compelled to take. One such case was that of Dick Butkus. In his heyday, Butkus was one of the most feared and respected of all linebackers. He sued the Chicago Bears management, claiming that his knee had been irreparably damaged by painkiller injections. The court awarded him $600,000.

For sheer toughness, endurance, and willingness to play while bearing the pain of an unsurpassed number of injuries, no athlete has ever matched Jim Otto. Famous for the "00" number on his jersey, Hall of Famer Otto was All-Pro center for the Oakland Raiders for fifteen years. "I've had thirty concussions," he told a TV interviewer, "twenty-five broken noses, a broken jaw, nine knee operations, teeth kicked out, a detached retina. . . ."

Every joint in Otto's body is arthritic. He has to brace himself against the wall just to get into his trousers. Even with his playing days over, he has repeatedly had to undergo spinal surgery. The subject of a recent Home Box Office TV special, Otto spoke courageously of his suffering.

In Olympic competition, shooting up injuries is officially forbidden. No evidence is available on which to base a judgment as to whether it actually takes place.

THE "NONCONTACT" SPORTS

The more violent sports are not the only ones affected by the abuse of painkillers. A recent scandal at Clemson University involved the track team. Members charged the track coach and the strength and conditioning coach with handing out prescription drugs illegally to runners who were hurting.

The runners were given anti-inflammatory drugs (phenylbutazone and Tolectin), which normally hasten the healing process so that athletes can return to action more quickly. But at Clemson, one runner died shortly after receiving phenylbutazone. Although South Carolina law enforcement officials said the cause of death was congenital heart disease, university authorities suspended both coaches, who resigned soon afterward.

Baseball, too, is affected. In his popular memoir *Ball Four,* ex-Yankee pitcher Jim Bouton recalls taking a whole range of drugs to ease the recurrent pain in his pitching elbow. He tried butazoladin, DMSO (dimethylsulfoxide), Novocain, Xylocain, and cortisone. "Baseball players," Bouton says, "will take anything. If you had a pill that would guarantee a pitcher twenty wins but might take five years off his life, he'd take it."

Wayne Simpson, pitcher for the Cincinnati Reds, started his career with a bang. He won ten straight games and thirteen of his first fourteen starts. Then he began to complain of constant pain in his arm. Over the next nine years, Simpson was unable to pitch consistently. He won an average of only four games a year. The team doctor could find nothing wrong. Manager Sparky Anderson hinted to reporters that the pitcher was just lazy.

Simpson allowed his arm to be shot up with cortisone. He kept pitching. One day his hand went white, cold, and numb. The doctor had to order an emergency operation to save the hand. Simpson later needed four more operations. His right hand was permanently disabled. He had virtually destroyed an entire artery.

Another nonviolent sport in which drugs are commonly used to enable injured athletes to play is tennis. In a book-length study of cocaine, Dr. Nannette Stone and several colleagues describe the case of a top-ranked player who developed mild but painful arthritis in one knee. Hoping to rid himself of it, the player took a year off and then returned.

The pain came back, too. The player's doctor prescribed Percodan, a powerful painkiller. It worked well, but the player found that it slowed him down and dulled his reflexes.

The player's manager then offered help in the form of a "cocaine infusion." This mixture consisted of pure cocaine diluted with distilled water. It was to be used like nose drops.

The combination of Percodan and cocaine worked marvelously. There was no more pain, and the player was sharper and quicker than ever on the court. He looked good and he felt good—until the Percodan wore off. Then the pain would return, worse than before.

For a while, the player rationalized his reliance on the drugs:

> Look, I'm in good company, you know? More than half the pros on the circuit use coke, and some of them do it just like I do—to compensate for the downside of their heavy pain medication. We all get hurt, but we've got to go on.

He added that many tennis pros use coke to combat the loneliness of constant travel, or just to build up morale when they're feeling low.

The player eventually began taking his "medication" off the court as well as on. Alarmed and depressed by this sign that he was on the way to becoming an addict, he called the cocaine hot line and got professional help. His chances of freeing himself from drug dependence look good.

7

THAT WINNING EDGE

THE AMPHETAMINE BOOSTERS

Imagine what it is like to gulp down thirty pills at one time. The result is a . . . five-hour temper tantrum that produces the late hits, the fights, the assaults on quarterbacks that are ruining pro football. They're at war out there.

—*Dr. Arnold Mandell, former psychiatric adviser to the San Diego Chargers, in* The Nightmare Season, *1976*

The incident might have been funny if it had not ended so tragically. It happened during a high school football game in California.

The coach sent a running back into the game, unaware that the player was high on amphetamines. The action began. The quarterback got the ball from the center and set himself for the handoff. The running back took the ball—or thought he did. He made a "brilliant run into the end zone," according to the *San Francisco Chronicle.*

Convinced he had scored a sensational touchdown, the runner was surprised to hear little cheering from the stands. Then he realized he had run all the way without the ball. Humiliated and ashamed, the youngster later committed suicide.

Amphetamines had a different effect on linebacker Steve Kiner of the New England Patriots. During one play, the ball was fumbled and rolling loose. Players from both teams were scrambling madly after it. Kiner just stood there dazed and motionless, his responses frozen by the drug. "I must have taken ten thousand beans," he admitted later.

A film of an Oakland Raiders game showed a veteran defensive end, confused by a high dose of amphetamines, going inside on every play. The opposing team kept breaking through for solid gains in the area that he left undefended. The player stubbornly ignored his own linebacker's signals and the insistent shouting of the defensive line coach. He was immovably convinced that the other team was planning a sweep to the other side. Nothing could change his mind; he had to be taken out of the game.

These are extreme reactions, but the drug's powers can still be unpredictable. Its specific effects depend on many factors, including a person's size and weight, mental and physical condition, and previous experience with drugs.

Amphetamines work on the central nervous system. Their effects are similar to those of adrenaline, a natural secretion of the human body. They get the body ready for action by stimulating the heartbeat and the rate of respiration, and by raising the blood pressure. Most pill-poppers report a surge of strength and energy, a sharpening of the senses, a quickening of the reflexes. They feel more alert, more confident, more aggressive. The pills give them what one expert has called "a jolt of get-up-and-kill."

Regular users are often rendered temporarily less sensitive to pain. Athletes who are playing hurt can often achieve wonders with amphetamines, despite their injuries. This might seem great if it weren't for the fact that they might also reinjure themselves and worsen the original injury— all without feeling a thing until it's too late.

Houston Ridge, a former San Diego defensive lineman, is one of the few who has won a court case over this type of injury. Ridge collected $302,000 from the Chargers. His suit contended that the Chargers staff got him "so high on amphetamines" that he didn't even know it when he broke his hip.

Despite such risks, amphetamines have been popular with athletes, coaches, and trainers. No other drug is so widely (and illegally) distributed in locker rooms and clubhouses.

In the summer of 1985, a series of trials in Pittsburgh had revealed widespread cocaine abuse among baseball players. Firm action was expected against all drug abuse by athletes. One panic-stricken baseball star was heard to ask another player: "They're not going to stop greenies, are they? How could we play this game?"

New York Times sports columnist George Vecsey tells (with some exaggeration) of the time he visited a pitcher in the clubhouse before his warmup:

> The pitcher was babbling a blue streak, and in my memory, smoke was coming out his nose, and maybe even his ears. I had never seen an athlete so wound up, and I raised my eyebrows toward a fellow reporter, who made a gobbling motion, hand to mouth. The pitcher turned in a shutout that day.

Vecsey recalls players joking about teammates who had taken amphetamines, were bursting with excess vim and vigor, but then had their games delayed by rain. They presented a hilarious spectacle as they tried to find outlets for their supercharged energy.

But the favorable effects of these pills can be counted on only when they are taken in low dosages, and over short periods of time. Complications arise when the athlete discovers that he must take increasingly large doses in order to get the same results. Harmful side effects multiply as the pills are taken in larger quantities, and as the dosage continues over days or weeks.

The bad results can begin with dry mouth, fever, and sweating. Vision begins to blur, coordination gets sloppy, concentration slips. Attacks of dizziness are not unusual. Friends and teammates may be startled by sudden swings of mood, from exuberance to irritability to depression.

Some amphetamine abusers have serious trouble sleeping. They develop a self-destructive pattern of needing pills to get to sleep at night, and amphetamines to get fully awake in the morning.

A Miami Dolphins trainer told Bill Gilbert of *Sports Illustrated* that

> some of the pros need almost a full week to get over being pepped up for Sunday. Afterward, they must have either tranquilizers or whiskey to bring them down. So they move through a cycle: pepped up, drunk, hung over, depressed, and then pepped up again.

Very high doses can bring on scary visions. Individuals who have taken a lot of pills over several days commonly develop the delusion that swarms of insects are crawling over their skin. They may also experience an alarmingly rapid or irregular heartbeat. Easily recognizable by the dilated pupils of their eyes, many amphetamine junkies develop a compulsion to repeat the same bizarre behavior for hours: folding and unfolding items of clothing, pacing up and down a limited space.

The harrowing side effects of amphetamines are more than matched by another popular performance-enhancer: anabolic steroids. Yet athletes keep taking both, trading off the presumed benefits against the damage to their health.

THE STEROID BOOSTERS

Dr. Bob Goldman is the holder of several world records in weightlifting and other strength sports. When he was a senior in medical school, he took seven years off to coauthor an exhaustive scientific study of the effects of steroids and other performance-enhancing drugs. Goldman published his results in a 1984 book, *Death in the Locker Room: Steroids and Sports.*

At one point in his research, Goldman asked 198 world-class weightlifters, discus throwers, shotputters, and other field competitors: "If I had a magic drug that was so fantastic that if you took it once you would win every competition for the next five years, but it had one minor drawback—it would kill you five years after you took it—would you still take the drug?"

To his astonishment, over one hundred of the athletes, or 52 percent, said yes. Dr. Goldman realized that both his question and their answers were only hypothetical. But the athletes' obsession with winning convinced him they really would do it if they ever got the chance.

There actually exists a category of pills that many athletes believe are almost as "magic" and "fantastic" as the one in Dr. Goldman's query. These are the anabolic steroids. *Anabolic* means "body-building." *Steroids* is a term describing their chemical nature.

Formerly derived mainly from the natural male hormone testosterone, most of the steroids in use today are manufactured by a synthetic process and sold under trade names such as Dianabol, Anavar, Anadrol, and Deca-Durabolin.

Coaches, trainers, physicians, and athletes who believe in the powers of steroids say that they increase muscle mass and body weight, reduce the proportion of fat in the body, and add significantly to strength and endurance. Taken orally or injected, the drug supposedly achieves these effects by stimulating the body cells to store abnormally large quantities of nitrogen, and by increasing protein synthesis in the muscles.

At least a million American athletes and physical fitness buffs, and probably far more, are using steroids today. The principal users are athletes in the strength and endurance sports: weightlifters; body-builders; hammer, javelin, and discus throwers; shotputters; wrestlers; cyclists; marathoners. Some experts estimate that more than 90 percent of these athletes use steroids regularly, and in large quantities. Somewhat smaller but still substantial numbers of football players, especially defensive linemen, rely on them, too.

Steroid use is spreading into the high schools and even the grade schools. In February 1987 the National Federation of High Schools estimated the proportion of high school students using the drug at about 3 percent—a low figure but an ominous beginning. National Football League consultant Dr. Forrest Tennant has reported that "parents of eleven-

and twelve-year-old players are buying steroids and giving them to their kids."

Sports that rely on finesse and eye-hand coordination rather than bulging muscles and brute strength see little or no use of steroids. Baseball is a good example. Steroids can hardly help much when a batter has to hit a three-inch ball thrown toward him at ninety miles an hour from a release point fifty-four feet away. Tennis players face a similar situation.

As athletes strive to loom bigger and stronger than their opponents, they take larger quantities of steroids. Retired world heavyweight powerlifting champion Terry Todd recently wrote that he had taken about 1,200 pills over a four-year period. Nowadays, Todd said, weightlifters take that many in less than two weeks.

A recent survey in *U.S. News and World Report* revealed that steroid abuse is widening in the high schools and colleges. Parents of some high school football players "have been told by their coaches that they are too small for big-time football, and have to gain 40 to 50 pounds." The parents are then advised about how and where to obtain steroids.

Dr. Robert O. Voy of the U.S. Olympic Committee wrote to the author of his concern about "13-year-olds being given anabolic steroids to build muscle and strength." This practice, he warned, "produces permanent cloture of growth centers in long bones and can permanently stunt growth. . . ." Such "manipulation" of young bodies shocked him both "as a parent and [as a] physician."

Bob Goldman became concerned about the possible ill

effects of steroids when an athlete who was a close friend died. Goldman immersed himself in a program of intensive research. He soon uncovered grave dangers inherent in long-term steroid use.

Goldman found that the drug could cause a rare type of kidney tumor, nearly always fatal in adults. It could also "inhibit growth in young athletes, cause high blood pressure, sterility, bleeding from the intestinal tract, and hypoglycemia; increase the risk of heart attack. . . ." The liver seemed particularly vulnerable to steroids, with liver cancer a possible side effect.

Dr. Voy wrote of the " 'time-bomb' effect of liver and heart disease from anabolic steroids . . . [which] can greatly shorten life expectancy." He believes steroids should be placed on the government's list of controlled substances, so that athletes would no longer have "easy access" to them.

Male sexuality is especially at risk with steroids, since the drug takes over the task of supplying the body with testosterone. This hormone, normally produced by the testes, is essential to male sexual and reproductive functions. When their role is taken over by the drug, the testes tend to shrink and atrophy. Impotence, sterility, and even cancer of the testes can be the consequences.

In a few unusual cases, the male endocrine system converts the drug into chemical compounds similar to estrogen, the female hormone. For these men, the tragic result is feminization. One of its symptoms is the development of "breast-eggs," or enlarged breasts.

Female athletes, too, face special dangers from steroid abuse. Derived from male hormones, the drug masculinizes women who take large quantities of it, or use it over long periods. The symptoms include unsightly acne, deepening of the voice, and growth of hair on the face and body along with thinning of hair on the head. Worst of all, the reproductive functions can be damaged, with shrinkage of the breasts and disruption or cessation of the menstrual cycle. In some cases these changes are permanent and irreversible, even after the individual stops taking steroids.

In an article in the February 1985 issue of the *Journal of the American Osteopathic Association,* Goldman reported that steroid abuse had killed at least six athletes during the previous year. Two had died of heart and immune system failure, three of heart disease, and one of liver cancer. There have been thirty-five cases of liver cancer linked to steroids since 1965.

Coaches and athletes feel compelled to use steroids because they are convinced that their opponents would otherwise gain an unbeatable advantage from using them. The pattern is particularly apparent in international competitions such as the Olympics. Athletes from the United States and other Western countries suspect that their brawny rivals from the Soviet Union and Eastern Europe are the products of scientific dosage with steroids and other performance-enhancing drugs.

"It's kind of like nuclear war," said Dave Laut, coholder of the U.S. shotput record. "We'll stop when you stop."

Shortly before the 1984 Olympics, female shotputter Lorna Griffin announced that the pressure to use steroids had moved her to decide to retire after the Games. She urged other female athletes to reject the drug also. Doing so might hurt in competitions against Communist countries, Griffin said, "but at least we are women, we will have our health, and we don't have to worry about our children being born with birth defects due to steroid use."

Advocates of steroid use claim that the most serious side effects have been reported only in a relatively small number of athletes. Their opponents point out that there is no way of knowing ahead of time which athletes will have the severe complications and which will not.

How effective are steroids, really, as body-strengtheners? The experts differ sharply.

The American College of Sports Medicine published an official statement on this question in 1984. It stated that steroids could contribute to an increase in lean body weight if the athlete had an adequate diet. The added weight might be largely water, however. The steroids might also contribute to small gains in strength. But the most important factor in increasing muscle mass and strength remained extensive physical training.

The *Physicians' Desk Reference,* a standard book about drugs that is used by many doctors, states flatly: "Anabolic steroids do not enhance athletic ability."

One of many strong supporters of this view is Dr. Melvin Horwith, an endocrinologist at New York Hospital-Cornell Medical Center. He challenges the claim that steroids cause storage of extra muscle-building nitrogen. Athletes' bodies, says Dr. Horwith, "are already storing nitrogen avidly." Any added storage effect is temporary at best, and "peters out" within a month.

Some experts believe that the benefits claimed by steroid

users are really "placebo effects." Goldman quotes former St. Louis Cardinals trainer Bob Bauman's amusing example of the placebo effect:

> I devised a yellow [Runs-Batted-In] pill, a red shutout pill, and a potent green batting pill. Virtually every player on the team took them. . . . They worked so well that we won the pennant. We used them again [the following two years] and again won the pennant. They worked because I never told [the players] that the pills were placebos.

In another case, athletes were given the steroid Dianabol and then asked about its effects. They all reported that it helped them a lot. Then they were given placebos—and they said that these helped just as much.

A specialist who believes in the strengthening and size-building powers of steroids is Dr. William N. Taylor, sports physician and a former body-builder and marathon runner. In his 1982 book he reports that steroids produce results only with trained athletes, however.

Taylor downplays the risks. In a view that is decidedly rare among physicians, he argues, "The short-term adverse effects are rare, mild in nature, and are reversible." As for the long-term dangers, Taylor sees these as "uncertain."

Taylor challenges the sports medicine organizations that have condemned the use of steroids. Why, he asks, do they insist that steroids are ineffective, while at the same time supporting expensive research for detection devices? If the drugs don't give users an advantage, why bother to detect them and punish their use? Such attitudes, he says, only help convince many that steroids must really be effective. The absolute ban on steroids also "inhibits further scientific investigation."

THE CHEAT-PROOF NEW TESTS

Athletes who feel that they must use performance-boosting drugs in order to compete on equal ground now face new dilemmas. Testing for drugs has become so sophisticated that users are virtually certain to be caught. The formal punishment is a ban from international competition for life, though the athlete can usually appeal this sentence and have it reduced to eighteen months.

The International Olympics Committee first instituted rules banning a limited number of drugs in 1967. In the years that followed, drug users were occasionally detected by the unrefined testing techniques then available. Today, over one hundred substances are on the list of banned drugs.

Tough new tests were introduced at the 1983 Pan-American Games in Caracas, Venezuela. They employed a new type of instrument called a gas chromatograph mass spectrometer, which is capable of detecting substances in concentrations as small as one part per billion. It can also pick up traces of compounds taken as much as six months earlier. The new machines are said to be "sensitive enough to detect a teaspoon of sugar in an Olympic-sized swimming pool."

Fifteen athletes from ten Western countries were disqualified in Caracas. One of these was the number-one U.S. weightlifter, Jeff Michels. He had to return the three gold medals he had won. Thirteen other Americans returned home without competing rather than face the tests.

The Caracas crackdown served as an advance warning for the 1984 Olympics. In the nine months before the Games, eighty-six American athletes failed the U.S. Olympic Committee's drug tests. They faced the choice of either coming to the Games in drug-free condition, finding some way to defeat the tests, or dropping out of competition.

The Soviet Union and its allies have long been believed to use the most extensive scientific research in the field of sports drugs. Their athletes have generally avoided detection as drug users. Nevertheless, they withdrew from the 1984 Olympics. Political reasons were undoubtedly the primary factor. But some Western experts insist that at least part of the reason was the Soviets' fear that the new tests were too rigorous even for their athletes.

By the time the 1984 Olympics were over, about 1,500 urine samples had been tested. There was one from every medal winner, every fourth-place finisher, and others chosen at random.

"Drug testing by itself won't solve the problem," says Dr. Irving Dardik, chairman of the U.S. Olympic Committee's sports medicine council. Athletes will sooner or later "find drugs that are not on the banned list."

Dr. Dardik urged giving American athletes the benefits of stepped-up scientific research. Scientists should "study how these drugs work and what we can do to help the athletes succeed without them."

Meanwhile, research is advancing rapidly in the Soviet Bloc countries. Their laboratories are said to have developed new uses for normally poisonous substances such as strychnine, and even nerve gas. These may serve as blocking agents that prevent the detection of steroids.

THE HGH BOOSTERS

The ban on steroids has led to an almost desperate search for substitutes. Most eagerly sought out are natural products of the human body. These are less likely to be detected by any known test.

One such potential substitute is the hormone that stimulates human growth. Its scientific name is somatotropin, but it is better known as HGH (human growth hormone). HGH is produced in tiny quantities by the pituitary gland.

Until recently, the main use of HGH as a drug was for children who were not growing properly. At present, HGH can be obtained only from the pituitaries of dead bodies. That makes it rare and expensive. New developments in genetic engineering, using bacteria, may make it possible to put larger quantities on the market soon.

HGH has drawn the attention of the sports world because it has the capacity to give athletes added height and muscle mass, strengthen bones and cartilage, and promote the use of body fat as an energy source. Its advocates particularly emphasize its alleged benefits to youngsters, whose bones are still soft-ended and capable of extra growth. The hormone could become the ''in'' drug of the future.

Some parents are so eager to further their children's athletic careers that they actively try to persuade physicians to prescribe HGH. ''I have received dozens of calls from fathers who want to make their average-sized children bigger,'' sports medicine specialist Dr. William N. Taylor recently wrote in *Newsday:*

> I've had offers of tens of thousands of dollars to chemically manipulate children. Parents have offered to fly their chil-

dren down to my office in Florida to have it done. . . . It could become a case of either take the drugs or don't play— you're not big enough.

The *Underground Steroid Handbook* touts HGH as ''great stuff . . . the best drug for permanent muscle gains.'' But the book tempers its enthusiasm with a warning that use of the hormone ''is the biggest gamble that an athlete can take, as the side effects are irreversible.''

The side effects can be shattering. One is acromegaly, a disease that Bob Goldman calls ''the Frankenstein Syndrome.'' The bones of the hands, feet, nose, and jaw grow huge, along with the soft tissue of the face (nose, lips, tongue). Often the heart enlarges, leading to congestive heart failure.

Continued use of HGH can also cause hypoglycemia and diabetes.

Dr. Taylor is one of those who have urged immediate steps to regulate the hormone's production, distribution, and use. ''By the time we determine [how much HGH] is more than enough . . . it may be too late to reduce, or cope, with the human suffering that . . . misuse will cause.''

THE BLOOD-PACKING BOOSTERS

Ten weeks before the Olympics trials of July 1984, U.S. cyclist Danny Van Haute had two pints of blood extracted at a San Diego blood bank. The blood was frozen and stored away. Shortly before the trials, Van Haute had the blood retransfused into his veins. He performed spectacularly well and easily made the U.S. Olympic team.

Van Haute's teammates soon learned about his secret. By that time there were only three weeks left before the Olympics. That left not enough time to follow his example in every detail. It takes the human body from five to six weeks to replace blood that has been removed. Trying to use their own blood, as Van Haute did, would have left them still in a weakened condition when the Games started.

Seven of the team's twenty-four members agreed to be transfused. The best they could do was to get blood from relatives whose blood closely matched their own. One cyclist got it from his wife. Others later told reporters that the coaches had exerted considerable pressure on them to do it. Team manager Mike Fraysse made no secret of his motives: "We weren't gonna fall behind the Russians or East Germans any more."

The cycling team rolled up the best record of any of the American teams, winning nine medals including four gold.

The procedure is called "blood-packing," "blood-boosting," or "blood-doping." It allegedly builds up athletes' strength and stamina by increasing the number of red blood cells, which carry oxygen. Higher levels of oxygen in the blood enable the human body to work harder for longer periods of time.

Some experts estimate that blood-packing can improve performance by fully 5 percent. A full year of training usually gives a benefit of only 2 to 3 percent. The procedure has the additional advantage of not leaving any detectable traces.

It also carries definite risks. Infection with such major diseases as hepatitis and AIDS, and severe allergic reactions, are among the possibilities. Some of the Olympic riders did become ill because of the transfusions. Three of them came down with flu-like symptoms.

Mark Whitehead had trained hard for four years. After getting the extra blood, he said,

> I got a high fever, 102, for two nights. I lost ten pounds from sweat and chills, and the day after that I competed. . . . It wrecked me. . . . But when you want to win, you do anything.

Dave Grylls was one of the cyclists who refused the transfusions. "I felt from the first day that it was wrong, that it was illegal," he said. "We were told not to talk about it to anybody except among ourselves. . . . Since it all had to be done on the sly, I think it was kind of sleazy."

After the 1984 Games, the U.S. Olympic Committee declared blood-packing "unacceptable under any conditions." The chairman of the medical commission of the International Olympic Committee announced in March 1985 that the practice would be officially banned before the 1988 Winter Games.

IMPOSSIBLE GOAL?

To ensure fair and equal competition in the Olympics— and in all sports—no athlete or team must be permitted to use drugs to gain an unfair advantage. Will this goal ever be attained?

Two factors are making it more and more difficult to achieve. One is the relentless advance of scientific knowledge. Research laboratories in many parts of the world keep producing new performance-boosting chemical compounds that challenge known methods of detection. The second factor is the athletes' boundless, often reckless, sometimes lawless determination to win. There seems to be almost nothing that some will not risk for victory.

8

THE WAR OVER DRUG TESTS

How should organized sports deal with the drug crisis? A broad range of proposals has been put forth. The most widely debated suggestion is mandatory testing. Athletes in every sport would be required to have their urine content analyzed. In some proposals, these tests would be done at regular intervals. Other proposals favor testing at random, so that the athletes could not know in advance when they might be tested.

Nowhere has the debate over mandatory testing waxed hotter than in major-league baseball.

THE COMMISSIONER VERSUS THE PLAYERS

Rumors of rampant drug and alcohol abuse by baseball players had been current for many months when the story broke wide open. In November 1983, three members of the Kansas City Royals were sentenced to three-month prison terms for attempting to buy cocaine. One, Willie Wilson, was the American League batting champion. It was the first time active players had ever gone to prison on drug charges.

Baseball commissioner Bowie Kuhn then suspended all three players for a full year. He dealt out the same penalty to relief pitcher Steve Howe of the Los Angeles Dodgers. Howe had been in treatment three separate times, but still seemed unable to stay away from drugs.

101

In the spring of 1984 the team owners and the players' union worked out a joint arrangement for dealing with drug-affected players. Any player believed to have a drug problem would be examined by a medical panel. If the three doctors on the panel recommended it, and if the players' union agreed, he would then have to submit to testing. Finally, if the results were positive, he would have to enter a treatment program.

While this agreement was being negotiated, a Federal grand jury in Pittsburgh launched a major investigation of drugs in baseball. The possibility loomed that a number of top players would be indicted and prosecuted. The new baseball commissioner, Peter Ueberroth, was deeply concerned that the game's public image might be badly tarnished.

In May 1985, Ueberroth announced a new program for mandatory drug testing. "We will include everyone," said the commissioner, "from the owners on down." Coaches, scouts, all other nonplaying individuals, even office workers, would be covered.

But for the major-league players, a separate agreement would have to be worked out with their union, the Major League Baseball Players' Association. In the minor leagues, where the three thousand players were not protected by a union contract, they, too, would be tested.

Ueberroth told a television interviewer that one of his main reasons for ordering the new program was to eliminate the chance of gamblers exploiting drug-dependent players. His goal was to attack the drug problem, he said, not the players.

The players' association reacted strongly—and negatively. Executive director Donald Fehr called Ueberroth's proposal "grandstanding." Fehr pointed to the existing joint drug program. "It's working," he said. "We've always felt that mandatory testing was demeaning." It "violates the individual rights of the player."

Fehr explained his objections during his interview with me. A relatively small number of baseball players have been using drugs, he feels. But "the public thinks a lot of players have drug problems." That puts all players under suspicion, so all would have to take drug tests. "Failure to take the tests would be construed as an admission of guilt."

What kind of country do we want to live in? Do we want to take steps that . . . put people on the defensive, that subject them to search and seizure without cause, just because they work in a particular occupation? Do we want to force people to testify against themselves? . . . In this country, you're supposed to have evidence against individuals before you accuse them of anything.

Fehr admitted that there might be good reasons for imposing special requirements on people whose jobs affect others' safety, such as airline pilots, police officers, even ordinary citizens when they seek a license to drive. But those reasons could hardly apply to athletes.

"I don't care," Fehr concluded, "if all the players in the major leagues want to go to Times Square and be tested there six times a day. But I do care if somebody says that being tested because you look funny today is a condition of your employment."

Support for the baseball players in their rejection of the tests came from the New York Civil Liberties Union. Norma Rollins, director of its privacy project, said mandatory testing "clearly violates the principle . . . that no one shall be searched without probable cause. In this kind of testing, everybody is searched. . . . It's a search without wrongdoing."

Most of the team owners expressed immediate support for the commissioner's proposal. They feared loss of public confidence in their teams. The owners also argued that the large salaries they paid the players gave them the right to insist on testing.

Additional encouragement came from the umpires' association. Its board of directors voted unanimously to join the mandatory testing program.

The dispute over testing is not new; it has been going on for nearly twenty years. As early as 1969, *Sports Illustrated* writer Bill Gilbert pointed out several ways in which athletes' liberties were already curtailed:

> Athletes customarily take physical exams, swear to their amateur status . . . are declared ineligible in many sports if they gamble, beat up referees or fail [academic studies]. In comparison to these matters, submitting to a drug test should not amount to cruel or unusual punishment.

Advocates of testing could also point to other activities in which the law requires physical examinations of various kinds. Couples wishing to marry have to take blood tests. Applicants for drivers' licenses have to take eye tests. Airplane pilots, locomotive engineers, and bus drivers are routinely examined, with urinalysis an accepted part of the exam.

While the deadlock between the commissioner and the players' union continued, the Pittsburgh grand jury concluded its hearings. It indicted several drug dealers who had gained access to the Pirates' clubhouse. At the ensuing trial, seven players, including some of the top names in baseball, testified under grants of immunity from prosecution. They admitted buying and using cocaine over long periods, and implicated about a dozen other players.

Ueberroth felt that the trial's revelations had further damaged baseball in the eyes of the public, and that he had to act to eliminate the impression that nothing was being done to clean up the problem. Ueberroth decided to try a personal appeal to the players. He wrote a letter, which was hand delivered to all 650 of them, asking them to agree to be tested three times in each season. "Baseball is in trouble," it began. "The shadow that drugs have cast on the game grows darker by the day. . . . It is our responsibility . . . to stop this menace before more damage is done. . . ."

Some of the individual players, and a few of the teams voting together, accepted the principle of mandatory testing. At the same time, they insisted that such a program could not depend on individual responses to the commissioner's letter. It must be negotiated through the union. The union's leaders accused the commissioner of attempting to bypass the normal processes of collective bargaining.

The result was another deadlock. This time, it was the twenty-six major-league team owners who broke things loose. In October 1985, they voted unanimously to terminate the joint drug program they had worked out eighteen months earlier with the players' association.

The owners' new strategy became apparent a few weeks later. They announced that any guaranteed contract offered to any player in the future must include a clause in which the player agreed to submit to drug testing.

Under a guaranteed contract, a player is paid whether or not he plays for the full term of the contract. The player benefits by being assured of security in his job for as long as the contract runs. Guaranteed contracts are common in the major leagues, especially in cases where they extend over a period of several years. The owners' plan stipulated that the contract for any player who refused the drug-test clause would not be guaranteed.

The players' association immediately denounced the plan as another attempt to evade collective bargaining. It pledged to file legal challenges to any contracts that included the disputed clause. An arbitrator subsequently ruled that drug-test clauses are "unenforceable," unless approved by the union.

But in January 1986, the Baltimore Orioles became the first baseball team to volunteer for a one-year pilot program of testing. Shortly afterward, the management of the Cincinnati Reds announced that all players signing one-year contracts were being asked to agree to a random-testing clause. Then the players' association formed a committee to see if a new voluntary testing program could be worked out for all the players.

Slowly and reluctantly, major-league baseball seemed to

be moving toward acceptance of testing in some form. By the spring of 1986, an estimated 400 of the leagues' 650 players had drug-testing clauses in their contracts. The question was whether the program would be jointly developed by management and the union, as had formerly been the case, or would be imposed from the top.

TESTING THE OTHER PROS

The situation was different in pro basketball, football, hockey, boxing, tennis, and horse racing.

Back in September 1983, the National Basketball Players Association reached agreement with NBA officials on an antidrug policy that was flexible but tough. Drug-dependent players who came forward voluntarily and asked for counseling and treatment would not be penalized. Their problem would be kept confidential. Their teams would pay for their rehabilitation, and they would suffer no loss of salary.

A player who had still not shaken his drug habit after treatment, and who again admitted to his problem, would be suspended without pay while undergoing a second rehabilitation program. The toughest part of the new plan provided that any player who had a third bout with drugs would be banned from basketball for life.

Also to be banned permanently were three other categories of players: those who refused to take drug tests; those discovered by the NBA's security investigators or law enforcement authorities to be using cocaine or heroin; and those arrested and convicted of, or pleading guilty to, using or dealing these drugs. Players could appeal the ban, but only after a minimum of two years.

This was the first agreement in professional sports in which players agreed to drug tests, and to such severe penalties. A major factor in persuading them was a section of the agreement that protected their rights while under investigation. For example, they had to be informed of the exact charges against them, and they could be represented by attorneys at any stage of the proceedings.

In marked contrast to the situation in baseball, it was the basketball players rather than the team owners who proposed this hard-hitting approach. The Milwaukee Bucks' Bob Lanier, president of the union, explained the players' feelings:

> We as a group were being tarnished with the brush of "all being hopheads," an unfortunate and untrue stigma. The overwhelming number of our players are not users of drugs, and once and for all we want to be able to convince the public. . . .

In the years since that announcement, the policy has been applied with some leniency. Several well-known players have admitted to addiction and have sought treatment— some more than once. They have been allowed to rejoin their teams as long as they remained drug-free. Only a very few, who proved unable to resist the drug craving even after going through two treatment sessions, have been dropped. The lifetime ban against players who have run afoul of the law remains fully in effect.

In the National Football League, disciplinary action against drug-affected players has been a practice of long standing. As early as 1974, the San Diego Chargers, their general manager, and eight players were fined for drug violations. Another example was NFL commissioner Pete Rozelle's suspension of four players, from three different teams, for part of the 1983 season. All had pleaded guilty in court to buying and using cocaine.

A "Drug Notice" posted in every NFL locker room makes the league's official policy clear. It warns that penalties for drug violations "may include fines, suspension from the League, and/or NFL probation." Players can also be required to enter treatment and rehabilitation programs. But the notice invites voluntary requests for treatment, stating that these will not necessarily "result in disciplinary action by the commissioner."

Rozelle explained: "If a player comes forward to his club, or goes honestly to Hazelden [a Minnesota drug treatment center that specializes in rehabilitating athletes] . . . there is no discipline." Only players who try to conceal their problem and are then exposed by security agents, or who become involved with law enforcement, are subject to punitive action.

The football players' union had supported these policies. But it agreed with the baseball players in opposing mandatory or random drug tests. Said union chief Gene Upshaw: "It puts the burden of proof on the players." Under the agreement between the union and the NFL that lasted until 1986, players were tested for drugs during their first physical exam before the beginning of the season. They could be compelled to submit to a second test only if the team management felt there was "reasonable cause" for suspicion.

By 1986, Rozelle was convinced that the drug problem was worse than at any time during his twenty-six-year tenure as NFL commissioner. He was particularly outraged by the revelations concerning the New England Patriots, humiliated losers in the Super Bowl by a lopsided 46–10 score.

Rozelle tried to get the team owners and players' union to agree on a new testing program. When that proved impossible, he unilaterally announced a new program to be run by the NFL. Entire teams, selected at random, would be tested twice each season at times not previously announced. Any player testing positively would either have to enter a hospital for at least thirty days of treatment, or would be treated as an outpatient, depending on the severity of his dependence. The player would be on half-pay. A second offense would mean a second treatment session without pay. If caught using drugs a third time, the player could be banned for life, though he could appeal for reinstatement after one year.

The players' union immediately filed suit and obtained a court order halting the program for a period of sixty days. Meanwhile, the issue was submitted to arbitration. But experts predicted that the conflict would drag on for years, embittering relations between the players, the owners, and the NFL.

The owners had long favored mandatory and random testing, so their acceptance seemed certain. The union's response was skeptical. Most of the players saw no reason to undergo more tests. Los Angeles Rams cornerback Gary Green spoke for many: "There's nothing wrong with the system we have now. The guys who need help can seek help. . . . The percentage of drug use is smaller in the NFL than it is in the rest of society.''

In hockey, no formal agreements regarding drugs existed until recently. The NHL has always taken an extremely hard line, threatening to expel any player caught using drugs or dealing them. That may be why so few hockey players seem to get into the drug scene. Until recently, when and if a player did develop a problem, it was dealt with quietly on an individual basis.

But in May 1986, league president John Ziegler and Alan Eagleson, executive director of the NHL Players' Association, announced a new testing plan. The league and the union would supervise it jointly. Players would be subject to mandatory, random tests.

Tennis, with its public image as a sport for the elite, was not widely known as having a drug problem. Apparently, fewer players were abusing drugs than in most other sports. Insiders were aware, however, that abuse of cocaine, heroin, and amphetamines was on the increase among the players.

In November 1985, the Men's International Professional Tennis Council unanimously adopted mandatory, confidential testing. The council is the ruling body of professional tournament tennis for males. Its spokesman said that the testing proposal had been recommended by the players themselves through their union, the Association of Tennis Professionals.

John McEnroe, the world's second-ranked player, was among those who favored the plan: ''Doping is not a problem in tennis, but by doing this, we will prove it. It will be good for tennis in the long run.''

Testing began in 1986. It was to be carried out at random at any two of the five most important tournaments during any calendar year. Players whose test results showed that they were using drugs would be allowed to seek counseling and treatment. Any who refused the tests risked suspension.

Female tennis players were not covered by the new rule. Their organization has not yet voted on the testing issue.

The boxing world takes a completely different approach. It is governed by state authorities, who make and enforce rules that are backed up by the force of law. There is no such thing as a prizefighters' union or a collective bargaining agreement.

How this system works was demonstrated in New Jersey in September 1985. Under a rule that went into effect at the start of the year, all boxers scheduled to fight in New Jersey had to be tested. The tests were performed on the day before each fight, and immediately after the fight.

About one thousand fighters were tested. Forty-four failed the test. The best known was Hector "Macho" Camacho, the World Boxing Council lightweight champion. He and forty others were suspended for ninety days. Four others were suspended indefinitely, having failed the tests twice. Boxing authorities in New York and Nevada, both important states in the fight game, agreed to observe the New Jersey suspensions. New York had long enforced its own rule, with annual tests for all fighters and random tests before fights.

In January 1986, fighting in Atlanta, Tim Witherspoon won the WBA heavyweight title from Tony Tubbs. A post-fight drug test revealed traces of marijuana in his system.

The Georgia Boxing Commission put Witherspoon on a year's probation. He would have to submit to regular tests and give antidrug talks to youngsters around the state. Failure to comply would result in the loss of his prizefighting license. Other states were certain to observe the Georgia ruling.

Like boxing, horse racing is regulated by the states. The sport has long banned the doping of horses, but in recent years, the possibility of drug abuse by jockeys has come under investigation.

On April 1, 1985, the New Jersey Racing Commission launched a program of mandatory random drug tests for jockeys. A group of top jockeys, including Angel Cordero and Bill Shoemaker, filed suit in Federal court to have the testing stopped. Their attorney called the tests a violation of "the sanctity of the human body," and of the Constitution's protections against invasion of privacy. "The courts have traditionally drawn a line around your body," he argued, adding that the tests were "more intrusive" than some body searches that had already been ruled unconstitutional.

New Jersey's deputy attorney general replied that the tests had been imposed by officials "solely interested in the safety of racing." All test results would be kept confidential.

In the first court hearing on this dispute, a Federal judge upheld the constitutionality of the testing program. He ruled that the state had a "legitimate safety interest" in requiring jockeys to be tested. As the case moved on to the higher courts, it was watched closely by officials in other sports. But in July a Federal appeals court upheld the constitutionality of the testing program.

TESTING THE AMATEURS

By the mid-1980s, drug problems among college athletes had reached alarming proportions. Responding to the worsening situation, the NCAA adopted its first national drug-testing plan in 1986. College athletes would be tested for seventy-nine specific substances, ranging from the "street drugs" such as marijuana, amphetamines, and cocaine, to the anabolic steroids. Testing would be done at all NCAA championships (basketball, track and field, gymnastics, baseball, swimming), as well as at the football bowl games.

Penalties were spelled out for athletes whose tests were positive, and for coaches and other staff members who helped athletes get drugs. The athletes would be banned from competition for ninety days. Repeat offenders would be declared ineligible for a full season.

The new program was expensive. Each test cost about $200. Only the medal winners at championship events, plus one or two others chosen at random, would be tested. In football and basketball, urine samples would be taken from a majority, not all, of the players on the top teams.

The new policy had hardly been adopted before the NCAA showed how serious it was. When tests indicated that the University of Oklahoma's top football star, linebacker Brian Bosworth, had been taking steroids, he was barred from playing in the 1987 Orange Bowl game. Despite anguished protests from Bosworth and his supporters, the ban was upheld. Athletes at several other colleges suffered the same suspension when their tests, too, proved positive for steroids.

"It's long overdue," said John Toner, chairman of the

NCAA drug committee. "We're not trying to solve society's problems, but at the same time we're not going to hide our heads in the sand. . . . We think there is enough evidence that there is substance abuse among our athletes."

Some colleges had not waited for the NCAA decision. By November 1985, ninety-six of the NCAA's 283 Division I colleges had begun some form of testing. Twenty-one had established drug-education programs. Another forty-five were studying plans for testing.

At the colleges that were testing, there were few protests from the athletes. Many who looked forward to careers in pro sports were glad to have their reputations cleared. They knew that college athletes suspected of drug involvement were often turned down by the pros.

Athletes entering college on athletic scholarships had little choice. They were informed that when they accepted the scholarships, they were at the same time accepting the drug tests.

Critics of collegiate drug testing contend that it discriminates against athletes. "Colleges could never get away with testing the entire student body," says Duke University law professor John Weistart. "But because there is no single party representing athletes, the NCAA can ride roughshod over their civil liberties."

TESTING AT THE OLYMPICS

The biggest drug problem at the Olympics has been the use of performance-enhancing drugs such as amphetamines and steroids, rather than escapist drugs like marijuana and cocaine. Concern about booster drugs had been building since the 1952 Winter Games, when hypodermic needles and empty ampules were found in dressing rooms. Steroid use had become so notorious by the time of the 1968 Games that the International Olympic Committee banned them that year, along with a long list of other drugs.

The first tests for steroids were done at the Montreal Olympic Games in 1976. Six competitors were disqualified. The available testing techniques were not very refined, and athletes were tested in only a few sports.

At that time, it was possible to evade the tests by stopping intake of steroids a few weeks before competing. The athlete would then take testosterone instead, which could not be detected. This would keep the athlete from losing any of the extra muscle power he had built up during the weeks or months on steroids. This loophole has now been closed.

New and much more sophisticated tests were introduced at the 1983 Pan-American Games. Between that time and the trials for the 1984 Olympics, U.S. officials tested athletes on an "informal" basis. They imposed no penalties on athletes whose tests were positive. Testing became "formal" at the actual trials, and eighty-six athletes were barred from competition.

At the 1984 Summer Games in Los Angeles, all competitors were forewarned about the rigorous tests. Few dared face them with drugs in their systems. The result was that only eleven of the thousands of athletes suffered disqualification. No Americans were among the eleven.

The U.S. Olympic Committee developed a rigorous new plan in the spring of 1985. It proposed to conduct random tests on American athletes at every major competition and training camp between the summer of that year and the 1988 Games. Athletes chosen for testing would be notified immediately after competing. They would have to report to the testing station within an hour and would be under observation during that time. Any athlete refusing to be tested would be automatically disqualified.

Those athletes found to have used banned drugs would be suspended for no less than six months after their first offense. If they were caught again, they would suffer a four-year suspension. That would mean they could not compete in the next Olympics. To be eligible for reinstatement, they would have to agree to be tested regularly during their suspension.

Testing all the competitors would be prohibitively expensive. Instead, the plan called for up to 1,500 tests each year. At the Olympic trials, the top three finishers in each event would be tested, with other athletes tested at random.

In a booklet issued to all athletes trying out for the Olympics, the U.S. Committee warned that "many commonly used medicines contain small amounts of banned drugs." These could cause a positive test. The same was true for many drugs prescribed by doctors. Athletes were strongly advised not to take any medication "unless it has been approved by the U.S. team physician."

The booklet tried to reassure athletes about their ability to compete at the world-class level without performance-boosting drugs. "Rely on your own talent, training, confidence, and determination," it urged.

The USOC's plan required approval by the nearly forty organizations that govern the individual sports. Approval seemed likely, since a refusal to cooperate could mean exclusion from the Games.

TO TEST OR NOT TO TEST

Should athletes be tested for drugs? There are strongly held opinions on both sides of this question.

A mid-1985 editorial in *USA Today* urged athletes to

> remember that with their renown comes responsibility. If they don't clean up their act they will corrupt sports. They will lose the faith of their fans. . . . The vast majority of players are not coke-heads. They should support tests for illegal drugs and work with . . . officials to devise fair testing plans that avoid abuses.

A leading force in the opposition to drug tests is the American Civil Liberties Union. It argues that performance on the field should be the basis for judging a player's fitness. Urine tests measure neither the player's performance nor how impaired or intoxicated he may be at the time when he is tested. "Tests should be limited to those . . . who are reasonably suspected of using drugs (including alcohol) in a way that impairs job performance."

To the argument that innocent people have nothing to hide, the ACLU replies that they have a right to privacy. "Urine tests are an unprecedented invasion" of that right. "There is a long tradition in the United States that general searches of innocent people are unfair. . . . Compulsory blood and urine tests are bodily searches, according to the U.S. Supreme Court."

The ACLU also notes that "the method of urinalysis most commonly used in drug testing (the 'EMIT kit') is inherently unreliable." It gives a false positive result at least 10 percent and as much as 30 percent of the time. The manufacturers warn employers to confirm EMIT results with other, more sophisticated tests. But these are expensive.

Urine testing, the ACLU concludes, "doesn't prevent drug use, or cure addiction. Education and voluntary rehabilitation are the only approaches that do."

A spokesman for those who challenge some of the ACLU arguments is Penn State football coach Joe Paterno. "An athlete has to give up that right to privacy," says Paterno,

> when he becomes part of a group that has to function together. If they are going to accept as much money as they get and the adulation they receive, then I think a coach has a right to know if a guy is physically able to do his best. . . .

Harold and Pat Connolly are husband and wife. They are also former Olympic athletes. In articles written for the *New York Times,* they expressed contrasting views on the testing issue.

Harold opposed testing in international competitions because he did not believe it would work. All the competing nations would have to cooperate, and he doubted that this would happen. Besides, scientists would always be able to develop "variations of the prohibited drugs" that the test computers could not recognize.

Athletes were constantly on the lookout for new ways to fool the tests. Connolly listed some known techniques:

> They take massive doses of vitamin C for a few days before competition to lower the pH content in their urine; they place a strong detergent on their fingers, get it in the urine to alter its surface tension . . . they use diuretics to dilute their urine or radioactive substances to mask the steroids.

He even told of male athletes who "actually had someone else's drug-free urine implanted in their bladder by means of a catheter." Some female athletes, he said, "have had specially designed urine-filled containers placed in their bodies, which can easily be pierced at testing time."

Connolly concluded that a procedure that drives people to such extremes does more harm than good to "health, ego, and conscience."

Pat Connolly cited the special problems of women athletes. There had been instances where male impostors had competed in women's competitions. By 1968, officials had devised a simple test to eliminate this fraud. A cell was scraped from the inside of the mouth, and a chromosome count then proved the individual's true gender.

Since then, female athletes have made extensive use of steroids and other strengthening drugs, despite the special dangers these pose for women. Pat argued that

> to establish respect and credibility in women's competitions and to eliminate the infuriating question, "Does she or doesn't she?" it is imperative that testing, particularly of

women for steroids and hormone levels, not only be continued but strictly enforced.

The widespread publicity about steroid abuse, Pat wrote, has cast a "tragic aura of suspicion" on the achievements of many female athletes "who have attained the results with talent, perseverance, and extensive training." She urged testing at least three times a year, "on a date unanticipated by the athlete, coach, or national governing body."

Harold Connolly's feeling that testing could never overcome the practical difficulties was echoed by Dr. Bob Goldman in his 1984 book, *Death in the Locker Room*. Goldman warned that testing inevitably sets up "a rat race between two medical teams, one trying to devise a test to detect the drugs, while the other attempts to mask the drugs or modify their chemical structures to make them undetectable."

But the sharpest comment may have been the one by ex-Dolphin star Mercury Morris, after his release from a three-year drug-dealing term in a Florida jail. Morris derided drug testing for "finding out there's something wrong with a guy's urine, when it's really something wrong with his head."

9
HIGH, HIGHER, HIGHEST

Relaxation, enjoyment, and a boost in self-confidence are the reasons why athletes resort to marijuana, hashish, and cocaine. They know—or should know—that these drugs have no power to improve performance.

THE MARIJUANA HIGH

"Pot" or "grass" is still very much around, though its use by teenagers seems to have peaked around 1977. Nearly one in five 12- to 17-year-olds were then smoking it regularly. Today the proportion is about one in nine.

The drug is more potent nowadays than it was a decade ago. The National Institute on Drug Abuse reported in September 1986 that marijuana growers have developed new strains two to five times stronger than those available in the 1970s. Teenagers smoking pot are more likely to experience extreme highs very quickly and suffer severe ill effects. They run greater risks than ever in attempting to drive a car while high or to play in any demanding sport.

When pot is smoked in moderate amounts, the high is usually experienced in two phases. Within about ten minutes, most users report pleasant, carefree feelings. This effect is technically known as euphoria. Their senses seem sharper, more responsive than ever. Their thoughts flow freely, though often in a wild and jumbled way. A distorted sense of time is common. Sometimes the user's perceptions of the space around him get distorted, too.

Then the smoker begins to feel more relaxed, often to the point of drowsiness. This second phase may endure for two to three hours.

Habitual marijuana smokers have been known to experience panic attacks, hallucinations, delusions, and paranoia. Also common is a loss of learning ability.

Marijuana is also harmful to the heart and lungs. The drug has a higher concentration of known cancer-causing agents than does tobacco.

Regular abuse of marijuana does not lead to a true physical addiction, as drugs like heroin and barbiturates do. But it can lead to a powerful psychological dependence. The result becomes painfully apparent when a heavy smoker tries to stop. His withdrawal symptoms may include insomnia, loss of appetite, irritability, severe depression, anxiety, and nausea. These conditions may last up to a week and sometimes persist in milder forms for a month or more.

Equally damaging in the long run is the loss of motivation that marks the marijuana addict. For athletes, whose success depends on disciplined training and fierce competitive instincts, such a loss is deadly.

Athletes who have trouble loosening up before a game may smoke a joint or two. But most are well aware of the way marijuana slows reaction times, blocks concentration, and blurs the senses. They avoid the drug before competing.

Particularly dangerous for athletes is the damage that habitual pot-smoking causes to coordination and reflexes. Any activity requiring a sure and steady hand, a clear eye, and swift and accurate responses becomes disastrously difficult for them.

THE HASHISH HIGH

An increasingly popular rival to marijuana is hashish, commonly known as "hash." This more potent drug is extracted from the same plant as marijuana.

Hash can be smoked in cigarette form, in the same way as marijuana. Regular users prefer smoking hash in water pipes.

The effects of hash, like those of marijuana, depend on the user, the amount smoked, and the quality and potency of the drug. The sensations it produces are similar to marijuana's but almost always a good deal more intense. The same is true of its dangerous side effects. Heavy abuse of hashish can lead to episodes of extreme mental derangement requiring emergency hospital treatment. In severe cases, the patient may have to undergo temporary physical restraint.

Hashish abuse is on the rise among Americans today. Athletes, too, seem to be turning gradually toward this more powerful drug in preference to marijuana. Close observers of the sports drug scene consider hashish as a potentially serious problem, but one not yet as widespread as marijuana.

THE COCAINE HIGH

Cocaine is far more potent—and far more dangerous—than either marijuana or hashish. It is rising in popularity faster than any other drug. Athletes of all ages are abusing it as never before.

A powerful stimulant that acts directly on the brain and the central nervous system, cocaine raises the blood pressure, heart rate, respiratory rate, and body temperature. The user experiences sensations similar to, but vastly more intense than, those brought on by marijuana or hash. He gets a quick burst of energy and alertness, a sense of almost unlimited physical and mental power, a "rush" of unbounded joy and elation.

But the cocaine high contains its own built-in trap. It lasts only a short time, usually from ten to thirty minutes. Then comes the "crash," or "comedown." The user is hurled from the heights of bliss to the lowest depths of depression, panic, and anxiety. All he wants, all he can think about, is to get back on that high as fast as he can. He will take repeated doses—called a "run"—until his supply is gone.

The most common method of taking cocaine is by "snorting" it. For a more intense high, the favored method is called "freebasing."

Freebased cocaine has recently come on the market in a form known as "crack." It is packaged in small amounts that can be purchased fairly cheaply—making it all the more dangerously attractive.

Because crack gives such a fast and intense high, it often produces an almost immediate addiction. The nationally known expert Dr. Arnold Washton declared that "crack is the most addictive drug known to man right now. . . ."

The drug's popularity has spread with fearsome speed. By the summer of 1986, drug-treatment programs in many cities were filled to capacity with people addicted to crack. The National Football League was so concerned about its rapidly increasing use by players that it called all team security officers to a special meeting for a lecture about the special dangers of crack.

Carl Eller, former All-Pro defensive lineman for the Minnesota Vikings, once had a $4,000-a-week cocaine habit. He only volunteered for treatment when he realized that opposing players were sneering at him, remembering his once formidable powers.

Now a drug consultant for the NFL, Eller has warned of the effects of freebasing. It builds up a "greater addiction" than snorting or smoking. Many players rely on it to reproduce "the incredible emotional highs they get on the field." Freebasing can give a player "the same thrill from coke that he got running ninety yards for a touchdown or making an incredible quarterback sack that saves the game. . . ."

Another NFL consultant, Ron Heitzinger, warns that involvement with cocaine often starts in college. "It is given to [athletes]," he says, "by users who want to ingratiate themselves, or by young women who want to socialize with them."

Addicted professional athletes go to great lengths to make sure their suppliers are always close by. That frees them from the need to carry large quantities of cocaine. The athletes make their buys before games for use during the games. Then they buy more after the games.

Alcohol and tranquilizers ease the players' comedown from the coke high, and help them to sleep. In the morning, they contact the dealer again for their wake-up high.

Some players try to save their paychecks by having them

sent directly to their agents. But then the craving takes over, and they find other money sources to spend on the drug. They may use the meal money they get when they are on the road. Or they may use the payments they get for endorsing products. Or they may turn to other players who are willing to share their supplies.

Both light and heavy users who snort cocaine soon develop the same easily recognizable side effects. Their noses get runny, they develop eczema around the nostrils, and the cartilage separating their nostrils deteriorates.

With heavier use of the drug, the effects get nastier. From being energized by coke, the addict goes to the opposite extreme. He has great difficulty sleeping and feels tired and depressed much of the time. He may experience a fast, pounding heartbeat, along with the terrifying delusion that ants or some other insects are running up and down his skin. There have been cases of cocaine use that ended in convulsions and death.

Dr. G. Douglas Talbott, consulting physician to the Atlanta Braves, has found that the player who uses coke "loses reflexes, muscle power, and visual coordination. All the while he thinks he's doing better than ever. That's the deadly trap of cocaine."

Dr. Mark S. Gold, who has counseled hundreds of athletes through his cocaine hot line, details some of the damage the drug does to their skills:

> Hitters have a hard time making contact with the ball. Pitchers lose something off their fastball and their curve and lose their concentration. Basketball players lose their shooting

touch and become confused during rapidly changing game situations. Football players have difficulty following the game plan.

Cocaine often stimulates feelings of hatred and aggression. Some athletes rely on it to get them into the proper "kill-or-be-killed" state of mind. The *Chicago Sun-Times* recently reported that coke-influenced players have been known to "rip apart their lockers while working themselves into an aggressive mental state for a game."

Athletes who become addicted make poor team players. Their selfish desire for the drug takes priority over their commitment to the team. Coaches, trainers, and teammates soon note unhealthy changes in the addicts' attitudes.

Tension may develop between the users and nonusers on a team. The nonusers may feel that their using teammates are not playing up to their potential and are letting the team down. The users may resent the nonusers' criticism and may fear that they will inform the coaches.

And cocaine does kill. No cocaine deaths were more startling than those of basketball star Len Bias and All-Pro football player Don Rogers. The two men died within eight days of each other in June 1986. The 22-year-old Bias, an All-American at the University of Maryland, had just been drafted by the NBA champion Boston Celtics. His future looked brilliant. He died after allegedly smoking cocaine in its potent freebased form, perhaps for the first time.

Rogers, a veteran defensive back for the Cleveland Browns, was one of the team's most highly valued players.

His blood was found to contain a level of cocaine five times greater than the amount needed to cause death.

Here were two young men, both in superb physical condition, both suddenly cut off by the deadly effects of a drug neither had had much experience with.

A noted rock star described to Dr. Mark Gold what cocaine addiction feels like. Many a star athlete could tell almost exactly the same story:

> I couldn't stop any more than I could stop breathing. I would crawl around picking up any grain [of coke] that might have escaped. I wouldn't take calls. I left orders that no one disturb me. . . . I stopped eating, shaving, washing, changing my clothes. I stank and knew I stank, but there was nothing I could do . . . except use up my coke supplies until they were gone.

One who would emphatically agree is first baseman Keith Hernandez of the New York Mets. Testifying in a drug dealer's trial in Pittsburgh in the fall of 1985, Hernandez painfully recalled his own years as an addict. He called cocaine "a demon . . . the devil on this earth."

Yankee pitcher Ron Scurry, another ex-addict, was asked whether players should agree to be tested for drugs. "It couldn't have helped me when I was on [cocaine]," he said. "At that point it wouldn't have mattered. I had to have it."

A Cleveland Browns player explained to former teammate Calvin Hill what made the drug so hard to resist: "Cocaine told me I was Clark Gable, Lee Iacocca, and Johnny Unitas all rolled into one. I liked that feeling. . . . Who wouldn't?"

Kareem Abdul-Jabbar tells of an entire pro basketball team that was "undermined by drugs." Five of its players were freebasing. He tried to talk to the team's star player,

> but he couldn't handle the simplest conversation and had to go slump in a corner so he could be supported by both walls and wouldn't fall. He was babbling like a man who had been in a prison camp. . . . They had been a good team but they had died.

In December 1985 the *St. Louis Post-Dispatch* reported that the NFL St. Louis Cardinals' losing season had been largely due to cocaine abuse by several team members. "There has been a ring of drug users on this team," one player told reporters. "The situation has gotten out of hand. . . ." Team owner Bill Bidwill ordered urinalysis tests for all team members as part of their postseason physical. Forty players accepted fines of $1,000 each rather than take the tests.

The high these players enjoyed was brief. The damage cocaine was doing to them, to their teams, and to the status and reputation of sports, would last much longer.

10
BATTLING THE BOTTLE

Pelle Lindbergh was 26 years old. He played hockey for the Philadelphia Flyers. He had recently won the Vezina Trophy as the National Hockey League's finest goal tender.

In mid-November 1985, the Flyers were riding a ten-game winning streak. Lindbergh and some of his teammates went out to celebrate. By five A.M., Lindbergh had had about fifteen drinks. His blood alcohol content was later measured at .24 percent.

In most states, anyone measured at .10 percent is considered legally drunk. At that level, most people's speech is slurred. They have trouble walking a straight line, or touching their nose with their eyes closed. At the level that Lindbergh had reached, most drinkers can hardly stand. Their coordination is a mess. They have tunnel vision, which means that if they are driving, they can only see straight ahead and are likely to miss curves.

Lindbergh owned a flashy red $52,000 Porsche 930 Turbo. Its listed top speed was 130 miles per hour.

When Lindbergh left the celebration, he was only a short way from home. He felt sure he could drive it. But as *Newsday* sports columnist Steve Jacobson wrote, "All the marvelous reflexes and depth perception that made Lindbergh a super goalie didn't get him home safely." There was a bend in the road, and Lindbergh missed it. The crack-up was total.

Miraculously, Lindbergh was still alive, but the damage to his skull had left him brain-dead. The doctors informed his heartbroken parents and fiancée that there was no hope. They gallantly agreed to have him removed from the life-support machines and to donate his vital organs to other patients in need.

Lindbergh's recklessness was part of a pattern of behavior that is typical of too many athletes. In Steve Jacobson's words,

> they are taught from a very early age that they are special members of society and its rules often don't apply to them. . . . Breaking speed limits is okay, drinking and driving is not beyond their skills. They don't have to deal with consequences as authorities too often look the other way.

Alcohol depresses the central nervous system. Moderate amounts give the drinker a sense of well-being. Heavy drinkers often go out of control. While under the influence of alcohol, and for sor¬e time afterward, the drinker's judgment is blurred. He has trouble coordinating what he does with what he sees.

As the drinking habit progresses, the drinker may proceed from ordinary hangovers to the more disturbing morning-after "shakes," then to blackouts, and ultimately to terrifying hallucinations (delirium tremens, or "DTs").

Long-continued drinking has been proven to be the cause of a host of physical disorders. It shrinks the brain, alters the functioning of the brain cells, and causes nerve damage. It has been linked to several forms of cancer. It leads to high blood pressure, stroke and heart attack, diabetes, kidney failure, ulcers, and more. Alcohol-related diseases account for between 30 and 50 percent of all hospital admissions.

Alcohol abuse is increasingly common among young Americans. It is the largest single contributing cause of teenage deaths, mainly in the form of drunk driving. The National Institute on Alcohol Abuse and Alcoholism recently reported that 3.3 million teenagers—nearly 20 percent of the nation's total—were abusing alcohol.

In another recent study, the state of Minnesota surveyed alcohol use among high school seniors, with special attention to athletes. The results were roughly typical for the nation as a whole. They showed that four out of five seniors had tried alcohol. But among the athletes, about 30 percent were frequent drinkers. This is a much higher percentage than has ever been reported for nonathletes. Problem drinking in the latter group has been measured at between 15 and 20 percent.

For no clear reason, baseball may be more heavily infected with alcoholism than other sports. Don Newcombe, former Dodger pitching star, an ex-alcoholic, and now the team's counselor for alcohol and drug addicts, estimates that 10 to 15 percent of ball players are chronic drinkers. A professional counselor to baseball alcoholics puts the figure at 35 percent. Doctors who specialize in this problem believe that no other occupation has a higher percentage.

An interesting explanation came from Donald M. Fehr, head of the Major League Baseball Players' Association. The circumstances under which baseball is played favor alcohol abuse, he said. The game is played in the thirst-provoking hot-weather season. The teams are on the road a lot, which leaves the players with a lot of empty, lonely time in hotels. They inevitably gravitate to the bars and cocktail lounges.

The public may not be aware, Fehr added, that beer is available in every major-league clubhouse. Some clubs are even owned by beer companies. Formation of a drinking habit is hard to avoid.

"With alcohol," said Fehr, "the players usually won't feel the damaging effects as quickly [as with other drugs]. The reason is that they're very young, and very highly conditioned. They can continue to perform a little longer, before the alcohol hits them. . . ."

But heavy drinkers are precisely the ones who have the greatest tendency to become abusers of other drugs as well. Baseball's drinking problem has by no means exempted it from other drugs. Cocaine, in particular, has been ensnaring ball players at a high rate in recent years and may soon surpass alcohol in popularity.

The alcohol problem does have one special characteristic. Drinkers' coaches, teammates, friends, and family often tend to take an indulgent attitude about alcohol, which encourages the habit. They treat the alcoholic as if he were a naughty but charming child, thus helping to retard his development as an adult. *New York Times* sports columnist George Vecsey made this point in his Prologue to the autobiography of Los Angeles Dodger pitcher Bob Welch, a recovering alcoholic. He learned

> that as long as Bob Welch was winning, his drinking was regarded as funny. . . . In my first ten years as a sports journalist, I saw athletes who gambled, drank, took drugs, had an overactive love life, and were rotten to their families,

all of which was tolerated by their teammates as long as they could perform in the game.

Despite all that is known about the harmful effects of alcohol on athletes' abilities, drinking has somehow gotten closely linked to sports in the public mind. The message that our society sends to the millions of sports fans—young and old—is that drinking is a normal way of having fun. For boys, drinking is presented as a way of proving they are real he-men.

Well-known athletes appear in television commercials and print advertisements, endorsing various brands of beer. The commercials are broadcast most frequently during sports events, when the audience is sure to include large numbers of young people. Advertising experts are well aware that the young are especially susceptible to this kind of advertising.

Broadcasts of such commercials have come under serious attack from parents' groups, educators, and many other sources. The commercials may eventually be prohibited, as happened some years ago to athletes' endorsements of cigarettes.

Whenever some top-ranked team has a big victory to celebrate, the TV cameras are there in the locker room to record the wild scene. Millions vicariously share the exhilaration as the players guzzle champagne and douse each other and their coach with it. A powerful message goes out: Success, happiness, and drinking all go together.

At least one well-known athlete has voluntarily cut himself off from the high income he derived from appearing in beer commercials. Bubba Smith, formerly a feared and formidable defensive end in the NFL, made amusing and popular TV spots for eight years. "I loved doing the commercials," he told the *Los Angeles Times* in September 1986, "but I didn't like the effect they were having on a lot of little people . . . in school. Kids would come up to me on the street and recite lines from my commercials. . . . It was scary."

Countering the media's message is not easy. One who keeps trying is Mark Heaslip, a player for the New York Rangers and Los Angeles Kings back in the late 1970s. He had the skills for a potentially brilliant hockey career, but a combination of alcoholism and cocaine addiction wrecked his chances. Heaslip had to quit the game after only three years. Even then, he was unable to break his drinking and drug habits for four more years.

Nowadays, Heaslip tries to give the benefit of his experience to young people whenever he can. "You have to make a responsible decision you can live with," he recently told a high school audience:

> How responsible is it to drink 12 ounces of beer and then puke it out? How responsible is it to drink and then get behind the wheel of a car and drive? Alcoholism may catch up to you when you're 15, when you're 20, or when you're 60 . . . but it will catch up with you.

Heavy drinking has "caught up" with all too many young athletes in the prime of their careers. In a few cases—Babe Ruth's was the most famous—it worked its destruction over a period of years. Either way, no alcoholic athlete has ever really beaten the bottle.

11
SHAVING POINTS

Sports gambling in America is this big: No one knows how big it is.—Sports Illustrated, *March 10, 1986*

For decades—perhaps for centuries—gamblers have infested the fringes of the sports world, undermining its integrity. Money and women have been the traditional bribes offered to athletes. Today, with so many addicted athletes, drugs have become the new and most dangerous lure.

Most American fans think of the great baseball scandal of 1919 as the earliest such episode in our history. The entire nation was in a state of shock. Banner headlines trumpeted the unbelievable news that gamblers had "fixed" the World Series. They had bribed several members of the Chicago White Sox to throw crucial games. The incident has been notorious ever since as the "Black Sox scandal."

Corruption was far wider in the college basketball scandal of 1951. Then, gamblers had bribed thirty-two players at seven colleges. Eighty-six games had been fixed in twenty-three cities over a four-year period.

Most seriously affected were the national champions, the City College of New York team. Only a year previously, CCNY had become the only team in the annals of basketball to win both the National Invitation Tournament and the NCAA tournament. Several of CCNY's finest players eventually pleaded guilty and were fined and placed on probation.

The 1951 scandal was the first to involve "point shaving." This is a technique used by players to manipulate the "point spread," the number of points by which a stronger team is expected to beat its weaker opponent. Point spreads are established by professional oddsmakers. If a bettor backs the favorite, he collects only if the favorite wins by a margin greater than the point spread. A bet on the underdog wins if that team loses by less than the point spread—or wins the game.

In point shaving, players try to control the scoring just enough so that the difference between the winner's and loser's scores is less than the point spread. Both players and gamblers prefer it to the old system under which players were bribed to lose games. That method was too obvious and often aroused suspicion (as it did in 1919). Point shaving, when done by skilled players, is much harder to detect.

The potential profits from such schemes are huge. In the mid-1970s, the Justice Department estimated the gross take on illegal sports gambling at from $20 billion to $25 billion. Today's best available estimates range up to $70 billion and more. NFL officials believe that pro football alone draws $50 billion a season. The total annual profit is probably in excess of $5 billion, about as much as the 1985 earnings of the Exxon Corporation, one of the nation's largest companies.

Much of this betting is carried on illegally, and much of the income produced by illegal betting enriches the coffers of the underworld. Mobsters are constantly probing for weaknesses among athletes that they can turn into hard cash.

A major scandal erupted again in 1961. Basketball teams

at Oregon, Iowa, North Carolina, and many other universities were implicated in a second point-shaving scam. Masterminding the conspiracy was Jack Molinas, a former All-American back at Columbia and a law school graduate. He went to prison for his part in the bribery.

As far as is known, drugs had played no part in any sports scandals up to this point. But over the next twenty-five years, drug abuse spread throughout organized sports. A nightmare loomed up: the likelihood that gamblers would sooner or later gain access to addicted players. Drugs would then become the irresistible bait that would ensnare trapped players in point-shaving schemes. Blackmail was another possibility, as players sought desperately to conceal their addiction from coaches and team managements.

Some sports officials assume that the enormous salaries paid to players in the pro leagues today virtually eliminate any chance that they would accept bribes. NFL commissioner Pete Rozelle sees it this way: "The only blessing about the crazy salaries players are getting these days is that they don't need the money they could get by fixing games."

NBA security director Jack Joyce agrees that the big paychecks "greatly reduce" the possibility of bribery. But he adds: "Of course, I'm not saying it can't happen." Joyce explained to *Sports Illustrated* how drugs are a new factor, creating new dangers:

> We've always been aware that if a fellow does get into cocaine heavy, well, he can go through $200,000 to $300,000 a year. So then the bad guy can come to him and say, "Why are you putting up so much bread for coke? Tell you what, we'll give you all the top-quality stuff you need.

All you have to do is give us two, maybe three games a year."

Top officials in other sports were equally concerned. "We've got to eliminate illegal substances from the game," said baseball commissioner Peter Ueberroth, "substances which can be used to control people." Ueberroth pointed out that the office of baseball commissioner had been created back in 1920 as a direct result of the previous year's Black Sox gambling scandal.

The nightmare became reality in 1979. Three Boston College basketball players were accused of point shaving in a series of games. This time, cocaine was part of the players' payoff. One player, Rick Kuhn, was convicted and sentenced to ten years in prison. His term was later reduced to four years. Another player was acquitted, while the third testified for the prosecution and was never tried. Henry Hill, the gambler and alleged drug dealer who was behind the scheme, also testified for the prosecution in return for lenient treatment. Hill said Kuhn had received cocaine and Quaaludes, plus $2,500 for each fixed game.

The Kuhn case showed how hard it is to detect point shavers. According to the FBI agent in charge of the case, no one suspected a fix in any of the Boston College games. Then, to the astonishment of agents who were questioning gambler Hill about a completely different crime, he suddenly blurted out the dope-and-dollars basketball bribe story. "Either you have somebody who confesses," said FBI agent Ed Guevara, "or you don't find out about [point shaving]."

The latest scandal broke in March 1985. It involved basketball players at Tulane. First to be arrested was the team's star, 6-foot-10-inch center John "Hot Rod" Williams. He had been named Metro Conference Player of the Year, was a member of the All-Louisiana college basketball team, and was considered almost certain to be a first-round NBA draft choice.

Williams and two other players were accused of shaving points in three Metro Conference games. They were formally charged with violating the Louisiana sports bribery law. Two of their teammates volunteered to testify against them, and were granted immunity from prosecution.

At the center of the scheme was 21-year-old Tulane student Gary Kranz. He was said to have made the initial contacts with the players. New Orleans district attorney Harry Connick charged Kranz with bribing them with cocaine as well as cash. The five players had shared a total cash bribe of $19,500, but that was secondary to the drugs.

The plan had apparently taken shape at the Alpha Epsilon Pi fraternity house on the Tulane campus. Two other students were said to have worked it out with Kranz. The conspirators expected to reap high profits by placing winning bets. To help in this part of the plot, they even brought in a professional bookmaker. The three students had placed bets totaling $34,000 on one of the fixed games.

As the scandal neared its climax, Tulane president Eamon M. Kelly expressed the dismay felt by many who like to imagine colleges and universities as sheltered havens: "I guess I thought we were immune from the problems dealing with drugs and bribery which impact our society at large."

Soon afterward, Kelly revealed that an investigation by university officials had discovered that coach Fowler had made cash payments to several players. Shocked and saddened by the multiple scandals, Kelly recommended that Tulane abolish its men's intercollegiate basketball program. The university accepted his proposal.

Most of the participants in the scheme pleaded guilty. They were penalized with fines, suspended sentences, and the obligation to perform community service for varying periods. Those who had profited were ordered to make restitution by donating money to charity.

Williams stoutly insisted on his innocence, refusing to plead guilty. "I have too much at stake," he told newsmen. His first trial, in August 1985, ended in a mistrial. A second jury found him completely innocent in June 1986. He was immediately picked up by the Cleveland Cavaliers.

Gary Kranz, centerpiece of the entire affair, was eventually granted a plea-bargain by the district attorney. In exchange for a plea of guilty to several counts of sports bribery, the drug charges against him were dropped. He was sentenced to serve three months in jail, pay a $45,000 fine, and perform 1,500 hours of community service.

The Tulane affair was at its height when the news broke that pro football might be the scene of still another drug scandal. Sports fans, already disillusioned with their idols, now read that an FBI report had accused five members of the Dallas Cowboys of shaving points in several early 1980s games, in return for cocaine.

Happily, it turned out that the charges were unfounded. The report had presented little supporting evidence. The

FBI supervisor who received it had deemed the report so weak that no action was called for.

The entire sports world breathed a sigh of relief.

Meanwhile, some coaches revealed their special precautions for protecting players from temptation. Georgetown basketball coach John Thompson is famous for his fatherly concern for his players. Commenting on the Tulane scandal, he asked, "Do you really believe those kids at Tulane are bad kids? They're my kids and your kids." Leaving them exposed to the rackets of gamblers and gangsters, he added, was "like throwing them in the Atlantic Ocean and telling them to swim." Thompson described his preventive plan:

> You know what we do? When we register in a hotel, we switch rooms, change keys, so no one knows whose room is whose. When someone tries to call a room they get the wrong one. You know why we do that? Because sometimes those folks who call want to throw games, want to sell dope.

Kansas State coach Jack Hartman told *USA Today* columnist Tom Weir that he, too, tries to keep his players' phone numbers a secret. But Hartman admits that "you can't isolate the kids. Basketball is only part of their life. You've got to let them be the student everybody else is."

Kareem Abdul-Jabbar recalls how his high school coach warned the players against the shady characters who hung around them. As the team's hottest player, these people tried to make him all kinds of offers. "I knew some of them were sharks," he says. They "would pose as college scouts in order to get next to high school ballplayers. They'd give them money or whatever a kid might be looking for. . . ."

There are times when the high salaries earned by professional athletes do provide a kind of immunity against bribery. Back in the 1960s, when a big-time gambler approached him with a bribe offer, Boston Celtics superstar Bill Russell turned the man away without a moment's hesitation. Russell pointed out that he was already making over $100,000 a year, and would earn well over a million during his career. "Now," he said, "to mess with you, I'd have to risk all that, plus my reputation." He couldn't possibly do it "for less than nine or ten million a game—maybe even more." No one ever propositioned Russell after that.

A different approach has been proposed by Vanderbilt coach C. M. Newton, who is also chairman of the NCAA men's basketball rules committee: "We could stop publishing the point spreads." Newton was referring to the fact that the point spreads appear in most newspapers and are openly discussed on radio and television sports programs. Newton is one of many observers who have pointed out that this kind of information only serves to promote gambling and to make point-shaving scams more likely.

Bucky Waters, former basketball coach at West Virginia and Duke, is now a sports broadcaster. He recently wrote that the person most likely to inveigle players into gambling schemes is

> someone very close to the team, familiar to them, from the barber shop or the social hangout of key players . . . someone who knows the weaknesses of the key players and has access to them. It is then easy to work on the weaknesses

or even create one for the targeted athlete: a dependence on drugs or even a threat to loved ones.

Are more drug-linked gambling scandals probable in the foreseeable future? Authorities at all levels, from high schools through the colleges to the pros, are now fully alerted to the danger. Law enforcement officials, too, are keeping a sharp eye on the sports scene.

But the investigative personnel and resources committed to this problem are limited. The NCAA's Gambling Task Force, for instance, is only a two-man operation. It depends for its information on the twenty-five investigators who conduct the NCAA's year-round, nationwide hunt for infractions of the rules.

Neither the FBI nor the Drug Enforcement Administration has any program for keeping athletes under surveillance. They pursue individual cases as these are brought to their attention. Both agencies do send out representatives, on request, to lecture the teams on the pitfalls of involvement with drug dealers and gamblers.

The most common form of investigation is run by the security directors of the various leagues. They have agents throughout the country. These are mostly retired FBI agents, who work closely with local law enforcement people. Their job is to alert the leagues whenever they suspect that a player is abusing drugs and in danger of being controlled by gamblers or any outside interests.

League authorities encourage individual teams to set up their own security departments. Several have done so.

Gamblers and their mob henchmen are well aware of the efforts being made to toughen security throughout organized sports. They know that they will have to proceed more cautiously than before. But where the potential profits are so great, and where the athletes' drug needs remain a point of weakness, the criminals on the fringes of sports are not likely to stop trying.

12

TREATING THE ABUSER-ATHLETE

The first three days, they put you in detoxification, in these pajamas, and I fell out of bed and I'm looking up at the ceiling, and I'm just saying, "Where in the hell am I?" . . . I'd have skyjacked a plane if I'd had a chance to, because it's a scary thing. You don't know what to expect. . . . And I'm saying "Wait a minute, I don't belong here." But I belonged there. —Former Los Angeles Dodger pitcher Steve Howe, 1983

Such were cocaine-abuser Steve Howe's alarming experiences at the beginning of his first five-week treatment program. He soon understood that he was at The Meadows, an Arizona center often used for detoxifying and rehabilitating alcoholic or drug-dependent athletes.

THE INPATIENT PROGRAM

The Meadows is one of several centers in various parts of the United States that offer inpatient, or residential, treatment. In this type of program the patient is committed to live at the center until he completes all the procedures. He has to abide by a set of extremely strict rules.

Inpatient treatment is designed for the most serious cases of drug and alcohol abuse. The typical patient is a deeply hooked addict who has not yet admitted to himself that he has an acute problem, just as Steve Howe insisted at first that "I don't belong here."

Howe had already spent $10,000 on cocaine before he desperately asked a friend to find him some kind of help. Before games, during games, after games, even once on a day when he pitched, he would go into the tunnel outside the clubhouse in Dodger Stadium to snort the drug.

Howe eventually went through treatment three separate times. Each time, he could not resist going back on the drug. He is now out of baseball, his brilliant pitching career cut short.

Patients committed for inpatient care are sometimes suffering from severe effects of their addiction. They may be experiencing seizures or hallucinations or episodes of psychotic behavior. They may have lost their jobs or be in danger of losing them. Their marriages and family lives have often been disrupted.

At the start of a residential program, the immediate goal is to bring the patient's drug or drinking problem under control. As soon as he is admitted to the treatment center, he and all his belongings are thoroughly searched. New patients usually know they will be barred from any access to drugs or alcohol from the moment of their admission. They often work out elaborate secret plans to "taper off" gradually instead of stopping all at once. Addicts and alcoholics can be devilishly clever about concealing drugs and liquor.

The patient then faces a long and exhaustive interview with one or more psychiatrists and other staff members. He will be questioned in detail about his personal, social, employment, medical, and drug histories. The interviewer will probe to find out how much of which drug was taken, under what circumstances, and how often.

The interviewer will also have to use all his skill and training to penetrate the self-deception that is common among all addicts—particularly among athletes. These men have often developed an astonishing variety of excuses to justify their behavior. They often arrive for treatment insisting that their performance on the field has been flawless, regardless of what the statistics show.

Staff members interviewing athletes have to be careful not to deceive themselves as well. They must avoid the tendency to idealize athletes, and thus to accept their statements about their drug problems. A psychotherapist confronting a man named the most valuable player in a recent World Series, or the quarterback of a Super Bowl team, needs to keep a clear and objective point of view.

Then comes a complete physical exam. If necessary, it will be followed up with treatment for exhaustion, malnutrition, dehydration, or other ailments common to addicts.

If the patient's craving still seems out of control, he may then be assigned to a locked ward.

At this stage, the patient is assigned a counselor. This person is not a professional therapist but has had training in the treatment of addicts. Frequently he is an ex-addict himself. The counselor will act as the patient's guide, friend, no-nonsense critic, and, when the situation warrants it, cheering section.

When another Los Angeles Dodger pitcher, Bob Welch, was admitted to The Meadows, the counselor assigned to him was an attractive 40-year-old redhead, Lynn Brennan. Always a great success with women, the boyish Welch tried to charm her. She ignored this and warned him that she could be very tough. In the ensuing weeks, whenever he tried to evade the rules or slack off on his treatment, he quickly discovered that she had told the truth.

The first five days are almost always the toughest. During this detoxification, or withdrawal, period, patients often go through agonies both mental and physical. Some get depressed and withdrawn. Many of them sleep a lot. Above all, they constantly crave just one more fix, just one more drink. "By the fifth day of detoxification," says Dr. Mark Gold, "the patient is usually so irritable and nasty that interaction with the staff is very difficult."

Medication and counseling are available to help with the most agonizing symptoms experienced during withdrawal. Alcoholics, for example, usually go through a three-stage withdrawal, each more severe than the last. The worst and final stage may include seizures, delirium tremens, severe agitation, disorientation. The delusions can be terrifying. There may even be outbreaks of violence.

Treatment for the milder symptoms may include sleeping pills for insomnia, milk of magnesia for constipation (a frequent problem with light-eating or malnourished addicts), and Valium for anxiety.

Patients require the closest medical attention during detoxification. In extreme cases, a real danger exists that untreated withdrawal can end in death, sometimes by suicide.

Bob Welch recalls that when he arrived at The Meadows, he was put into blue pajamas and a hospital robe. You have to wear these, says Welch, "until you're a good boy. . . .

If down the line you misbehave in some way, they put you back in the pajamas again.'' The idea is to make the patient aware that he is a sick person, and hasn't really started on the cure yet.

Welch remembers also that no matter who you are, nobody helps you with your bags when you arrive. You have to carry them yourself. For him, as a baseball celebrity accustomed to being fawned on and waited on at every turn, this was a bit of a shock.

Another early step in the program requires the patient to make a list of the bad things he's done while drunk. The purpose is to convince him that his craving really was out of control. By the time Welch had finished confessing to all his wild and ugly actions, he was in tears. His counselor reassured him: "I feel you have really gotten in touch with your feelings."

Once detoxification has been completed, the center's 24-hour-a-day structured program can go to work. Usually the patient will be required to see a psychotherapist for intensive individual sessions every day. The therapist will concentrate first on gaining the athlete's trust. Then he and the athlete will explore the causes of the addiction. Together they will try to discover ways in which the athlete can cope with these causes. Finally, the therapist will help the athlete to develop better attitudes toward himself and others.

The therapist will also sign the patient up to participate in group therapy two or three times a week. The group usually consists of from six to twelve people. It works best if the group members are all suffering from the same type of addiction as the athlete.

The group discussions are guided by one or two psychotherapists. Counselors, social workers, and other staff members may join in. The group members share experiences and compel each other to talk honestly and openly about their problems. Each helps the others to deal with sometimes painful truths about themselves. Since all have been through the drug or alcohol ordeal, it is very difficult to con them with fake alibis. They know all the excuses, having tried them themselves.

Patients attend many lectures, on subjects ranging from the effects of drugs and booze to family and other personal relationships. It was at one of these that Welch first learned that "once an alcoholic, always an alcoholic. You could be a 'recovering alcoholic,' but there's no such thing as a 'recovered alcoholic.' "

Some centers involve the patient's family in the treatment process at various stages of the program. Bob Welch had to call home shortly after entering treatment. He had to admit to his mother that he was "getting dried out with a bunch of alcoholics." He was expecting tears and scolding. To his surprise, his mother was pleased and offered encouragement. Welch broke down, sobbing. "That," he told his counselor, "was the hardest thing I ever did."

"Family Week," near the end of the program, was the most important part of Welch's treatment. The mornings were devoted to meetings not attended by the patient, at which his family discussed its relations with the patient.

The family met with the patient in the afternoons. The counselors guided the members toward bringing up everything that the patient might have done to them. They were encouraged to confront the patient with these acts as directly as possible. These sessions were often painful to everyone involved, but they produced valuable self-discoveries on all sides.

At his "graduation," Welch got up and spoke briefly. "I came here," he said, "trying to bullshit everybody and just get through the process. But everybody knew it, and wouldn't let me."

Most inpatient programs last about thirty days. According to Don Fehr of the Major League Baseball Players' Association, the only reason for this is that the insurance companies pay for that period only. There is no medical reason for such a short term of treatment. Many of the medical experts believe that, with problems as severe as those that afflict these patients, a longer confinement in a residential program would undoubtedly have more long-lasting effects.

Upon release, patients are scheduled into an aftercare program that may last from six to twelve months. They may have to continue with both individual and group therapy sessions. They may have to attend weekly meetings of Cocaine Anonymous, Alcoholics Anonymous, or any of the similar groups that have been organized in recent years. They will almost always be required to provide urine and blood samples at frequent intervals.

For athletes who have to travel with their teams, special arrangements can be made with therapists and support groups in cities throughout the country.

When Bob Welch returned to the Dodgers, he was unsure about the reception he could expect from his teammates. He had had some unpleasant confrontations with some of them while drunk. The first one he told about his treatment program was Hall of Famer Sandy Koufax, now a pitching coach. "That's great!" was Koufax's reaction. "Congratulations! Terrific!"

Then, at a team meeting, Welch stood up, admitted that he was a recovering alcoholic, and apologized to any players he might have offended in the old days. Every player on the team responded warmly and encouragingly.

With that kind of support, Welch won nine games and lost five that year. He was named to the National League All-Stars. At the same time, he was fulfilling all of his aftercare obligations.

Aftercare treatment is as essential for achievement of a genuine cure as the inpatient program itself. A dismaying number of athletes sooner or later become bored with the program or restless. Some convince themselves that they are cured and need no further therapy. They then break away from the aftercare routine.

The number who return to their former drug or drinking habit is tragically high. Federal scientists recently estimated that more than half of those seeking help for cocaine addiction eventually get hooked again. Even among those who stay with aftercare to the end, only about 60 percent remain permanently drug-free.

In the words of Dr. Daniel Begel, a psychiatrist who specializes in the treatment of athletes, doctors are rarely surprised to see an athlete resume his drug habit. The doctor

knows that the illness is in the person, not the drug. The athlete's problems, a bad marriage for example, will not improve because he is drug-free. . . . His self-esteem will not suddenly rest secure. Injuries will nag, competition will press, and drugs and the sex that sometimes comes with them will tempt. . . .

Dr. Arnold Washton, head of drug-abuse research and treatment at New York's Regent Hospital, points out that drug dependency is "a chronic relapsing disorder." Even the best inpatient program, he says, is only a beginning: "The real task of treatment begins once the person is back in his normal environment, dealing with urgings, availability [of drugs], and stress." Considering the kind of lives that professional athletes lead, "it is very surprising that some are able to successfully recover."

THE OUTPATIENT PROGRAM

For athletes who are willing to admit that they have a drug or drinking problem, but are less dependent than the most severely hooked addicts, outpatient care may be the answer. Under this type of program the athlete may continue to live at home or school, or even travel with his team.

The most basic requirement of outpatient care is that the patient immediately and totally stop drinking or taking drugs of any kind. Frequent urine and blood tests will verify his compliance with this absolute rule.

Stopping drugs is actually easier in the inpatient setting. There the patient is given no choice. He is simply deprived of all access to drugs. But in outpatient treatment, the addict has to make the decision and enforce it on his own.

Most outpatient programs last about six months. The prognosis for patients who stick to the program is better than the cure rate for those who have been through inpatient treatment. This is at least partly because most outpatients were more lightly addicted, and more honest about themselves, in the first place.

The actual treatment is similar to that given in the aftercare part of the inpatient program. The athlete may be required to see his psychotherapist daily, take part in group therapy, and attend weekly meetings of one of the self-help groups. Meanwhile, if his physical condition permits, he practices and plays with his team as usual.

But the routine may vary from one outpatient clinic to another. Depending on the patient's condition, he may be expected to visit the clinic only once or twice a week. Some clinics put the patient through an intensive six-week program of daily treatment, with a one-year followup or aftercare requirement. In some cases the aftercare may be open-ended, with the length of time determined by the patient's progress.

Some outpatient programs use special techniques to keep the patient off drugs. The Cocaine Clinic in Aspen, Colorado, is one of those that uses the so-called blackmail technique. The patient is required to give his therapist a signed letter containing the worst, most self-incriminating type of information. Such a letter might contain not only a confession about drug abuse, but might also describe some outlandish or even illegal act committed while under the influence.

For athlete-patients, the letter may be addressed to the league commissioner, the team owner, the coach, or even the newspapers.

The patient then has to submit to random urine and blood tests. If any turn out positive, the letter is mailed. The success rate so far has been about 90 percent.

Another method used in some outpatient programs is the contract. The patient spells out his goals and expectations, and promises to fulfill the program requirements as listed by the therapist. Then a list of penalties is added. For example: The patient comes in for an individual therapy session, and he is obviously high. He pays for the session, but has to leave immediately, receiving no treatment on that day.

Marijuana smokers who use the drug heavily enough to require treatment seldom need to be committed to a full-scale inpatient program. They can almost always benefit from outpatient care. Detoxification can usually be achieved in a few days. The withdrawal symptoms are far less severe than those experienced by hard drug users. Also available is the recently organized Potsmokers Anonymous, with chapters throughout the country.

When the marijuana patient is a young person, the family is usually brought in at an early stage of treatment to air and discuss the conflicts that are often at the root of the difficulty. Psychologist Miriam Cohen explains that the typical marijuana patient

> must first get psychological support from those in his environment—from professionals, and from his friends and family. The person must be taught how to tackle life's problems without the aid of a drug, and how to recognize his own emotional conflicts and negative feelings, and learn to deal with them in a more direct, productive way.

In the case of an athlete who has gotten into heavy pot smoking but has not yet gone on to harder drugs, the prognosis is often favorable. The trouble is that such cases are relatively rare. Marijuana is notorious as the "gateway drug," which opens the way to more serious drug involvements. Most heavy pot smokers have at least begun to abuse other drugs as well.

Few statistics are available on the results of treatment for athletes, whether of the inpatient or outpatient type. As far as is known, the results seem generally good. The percentage of athletes permanently cured is encouraging. But a substantial minority of those who have been through treatment—perhaps as many as four out of ten—still return to drug or alcohol abuse.

Treatment is a valid response to the problem. It cannot be the only response. Other approaches must be explored.

13

THE ULTIMATE DRUG CURE: PREVENTION

Drug tests will not do it. Street surveillance and stiff penalties will not do it. Elaborate systems of treatment and rehabilitation will not do it. None of these, separately or jointly, will solve the worsening drug problem. At best they may limit its spread and perhaps even reduce it somewhat.

For any real hope of progress toward a drug-free sports world, the primary emphasis must be placed on prevention. A comprehensive antidrug program is required to deal with sports in the schools, the colleges, and the pro leagues. It will work only if it emphasizes the health and well-being of the athletes above all. And it will have to avoid focusing only on athletes, as testing does. An effective program will include measures to be taken by coaches, trainers, and sports physicians; by sports administrators and policymakers; by parents and educators; and by influential leaders at all levels of American society.

PREVENTION FOR ATHLETES

Few groups in society depend more heavily on their physical, mental, and moral health than sports competitors. If life were logical, athletes could be relied on to take the best possible care of their own health. Some athletes—probably a majority—do watch out for themselves. They keep themselves in top shape because they know enough, and have

159

enough self-discipline, to eat right, live right, train right. Others are just lucky. They inherited their powerful physique, superb coordination, natural agility, superior vision, or speed.

Obviously, there are athletes who neglect or abuse their bodies. There would be no drug and drinking problems in sports if this were not so.

All athletes can benefit from instruction about good health practices and about the damage they can do to themselves through bad ones. Athletic training at its best has always included a good measure of health education.

When such education is conducted properly, it devotes as much attention to mental health as to physical. It recognizes that not all athletes are naturally equipped to cope with the stresses of competition. Psychological instruction and counseling are most effective when they start at an early age. They can be conducted in classroom settings, in group sessions with fellow athletes, and in individual meetings with trained counselors.

Some of the concepts that athletes need to understand may seem obvious and elementary. They need to appreciate, for instance, that their own self-worth as individuals is not determined by whether they win or lose. They must overcome the idea that is constantly instilled into them, that only winners are valuable human beings, while losers are shameful and pathetic.

Coaches, teammates, fellow students, the media, and the public all too often heap humiliation on losing players. Standing up to that kind of treatment requires great inner strength. That quality seems to be built in to some athletes.

Others, more sensitive or perhaps less mature, suffer deep psychological wounds. Their self-confidence can be repaired and strengthened through well-conducted counseling.

Athletes need strong self-esteem not only for those inevitable occasions when they are on the losing side. They need it for other constructive forms of behavior. It is never easy to say no to friends, teammates, or admirers who offer drugs or drinks. It is even harder to confront teammates who may be abusing drugs. But such actions are possible. They too can be learned and "rehearsed" in counseling situations.

Even athletes who have considerable experience with drugs and alcohol often know little or nothing about the substances they take into their bodies. Experts are available from many sources to give them the facts, dispel the myths, and explain the risks. Most of the pro teams have well-developed programs for visits by these people. So do many colleges and schools. But these programs will reach maximum effectiveness only when they reach all athletes, at all levels of competition. There is no substitute for accurate information.

"There is only one long-run way to deal with [the drug crisis]," says Don Fehr. "The athlete has to be highly educated about drugs very early on, and in a meaningful way. He must learn to make affirmative choices, for affirmative reasons, not to indulge in abusive substances."

The most effective speakers on drug abuse, says Fehr, are people the players can believe in and trust. Their presentations must be positive and encouraging in tone, "not threatening, not preaching."

Athletes get bored as easily as anyone else. Information about drugs needs to be presented in some dramatic way. Other athletes, or respected former athletes, or even athletes who are former drug addicts or alcoholics, are often the most effective carriers of the antidrug message.

Helpful in this regard is a broad five-year effort announced late in 1984 by the federal government's Drug Enforcement Administration. This "Sports Awareness Drug Program" is aimed at some sixty million students, from kindergarten through college. Athletes, coaches, and law enforcement officials are serving as lecturers and counselors. Well-known sports personalities star in ads publicizing the program throughout the country.

The FBI has also had a drug education program for some years. Its speakers are particularly well qualified to discuss the dangers of sports bribery as a part of the drug menace. They are available for athlete audiences at every level, from the schools and colleges to the pros.

The Major League Baseball Players' Association launched an innovative drug prevention program early in 1986. As a first step, the Association published a coloring book for younger children, titled *It's O.K. to Say No to Drugs!* It quotes popular players, encouraging youngsters to resist pressures from friends to use drugs. The players have been promoting the book actively through radio and television announcements and personal appearances. If this first book proves popular, later volumes will be targeted at older children and parents.

At the same time, the Players' Association set up a "pilot program of active involvement," with players spending time with schoolchildren. Members of the Kansas City Royals were the first to try this, with fifth- and sixth-graders of the Shawnee Mission school district outside Kansas City, Missouri.

Another fine source for materials on drugs and how to fight them is the Hazelden Foundation. This Minnesota-based organization runs a drug treatment and rehabilitation center to which many of the nation's top teams and institutions send addicted or alcoholic athletes.

Some Hazelden publications offer useful strategies for preventing drug problems. An example is the suggestion of "straight" after-game parties, where only nonalcoholic beverages are served and the use of alcohol or drugs is discouraged. "These parties," says a Hazelden pamphlet, "are sometimes sponsored by coaches or parents of high school athletes, but most often planned by team members or captains."

Preseason captains' meetings are another potentially helpful idea. These are usually held so that teams can discuss commitment, attitudes, and team policies or rules. They can also provide a good forum for talk about drugs and their effect on team performance and morale: "Athlete-to-athlete communication is probably the best way to send clear messages about chemical use."

For younger athletes, meetings with parents can also have positive results. They provide an opportunity for parents, athletes, coaches, and other school staff to discuss all aspects of the athletic program, including the drug danger. A valuable result can be the development of a bond of shared responsibility and understanding.

In some school settings, older students are trained to make antidrug presentations to junior high or elementary school students. The older ones benefit by increasing their own skills and knowledge, while the younger ones gain an additional source of information.

Hazelden encourages athletes to talk frankly to each other about drug or drinking problems. They must overcome their natural hesitancy about confronting their peers. "You don't have to be an expert in chemical use problems or counseling, to tell someone that you care about him or her and are concerned about what is happening."

The pamphlet warns, however: "You are not a counselor, you're a teammate." It advises against "bailing your teammate out of trouble repeatedly or trying to fix his or her problem." Instead, the athlete should encourage the troubled teammate to talk to some trusted and competent person such as a counselor, a coach, or a trainer.

PREVENTION FOR COACHES

Coaches can be powerful influences on their young disciples. They almost inevitably become role models. The personal goals, the attitudes, the values they express through their ways of dealing with athletes can leave deep and permanent impressions.

Some coaches have a natural talent for esteem-building interaction with players. They understand how crucial to mental health the athlete's self-image is—and how easily it can be destroyed by a coach's harsh criticisms.

Thoughtful coaches recognize athletes' needs for personal development in areas outside of sports. They take a genuine interest in the youngsters' academic progress and try to maintain a reasonable balance between their own demands and the athletes' studies. They accept the athletes' need for recreational fun outside of team activities.

Coaches are teachers, but the good ones extend their teaching well beyond athletic skills. They help players to understand the proper place of sports in their lives. They help train them to cope with stress. Above all, wise and well-adjusted coaches by their own example foster balanced attitudes toward winning and losing. That includes allowing injured players sufficient time for their wounds to heal, rather than pressuring them to get back into action before they're ready.

An effective way to help players mature is by allowing them a say in decisions that affect them. The more responsibility they are encouraged to assume for their own actions, the greater their sense of commitment will be. Too many coaches treat athletes virtually like children, on and off the field.

Experienced players can, for example, be brought in to help develop the game plan. At the very least, players can be allowed to lead certain segments of practice. Or, team members might be selected to devise one new drill each week. Whatever the specific technique the coach chooses, he will be contributing to the development of individuals less likely to prefer the dream world of drugs to reality.

Provided that they understand the sensitivities involved, coaches can exercise considerable influence over athletes' attitudes toward drugs. If they themselves dispense drugs improperly, that will obviously have a negative effect on players' attitudes. They can instead provide clear and consistent guidelines, emphasizing that no chemical has ever been shown to improve performance for very long, and that most will sooner or later damage performance, perhaps irreparably.

A fascinating conference on the role coaches play in athletes' drug and alcohol abuse was held in Long Beach, New York, early in 1986. A particularly impressive speaker was Mike Hall of the Forest Hills school district, Cincinnati, Ohio. A former coach and athletic director, Hall is the chief developer of a widely imitated model program for drug abuse prevention in the schools.

As the first step toward launching such a program, Hall recommends a school district survey of athletes' abuse problems. When he did this in his district, the results were startling. Two out of three senior athletes admitted using alcohol during the sports season. Over 90 percent of them reported that there were parties every weekend during the season, at which athletes drank. From 50 to 90 percent used alcohol once every week—every week of the year.

Those conducting the survey were especially disturbed by the athletes' report that there were few merely social drinkers among teenagers. They said that teenagers drink until they pass out or get sick, or until the booze runs out. The effects on their health—and their driving—are not hard to imagine.

Twelve percent of these athletes admitted using pot while participating in sports. Five percent admitted to other drugs.

But the most unexpected result turned up in the junior high schools. No less than 38 percent of these 12- to 15-

year-old athletes had used alcohol during the sports season. "This," said Hall, "is where the program must start."

Hall pointed out that some coaches actually encourage drug and alcohol abuse through gutless behavior. For example, it's not unusual for coaches to overhear their players making party plans that involve drugs and drinking. Reluctant to risk their popularity, the coaches pretend they didn't hear. The same kind of thing happens when they smell alcohol or marijuana.

"What a coach should do," says Hall, "is confront the athletes immediately and tell them that kind of talk and that behavior are inappropriate." He must seize the moment to show that he is genuinely concerned about them. Failure to act only gives the athletes the impression that the coach knows, but doesn't really care.

Coaches often avoid talking to their players about drugs altogether, says Hall. Some may mention it once, at the start of a season, and never refer to it again.

Other coaches simply deny the problem. Or they insist that "it's not a problem on my team; maybe on other teams."

Then there are those who fear to face reality because a drug problem on their team might be construed as a reflection on them. As long as they keep quiet about it, they think, no one can blame them.

Equally common is the practice of setting up rules against drugs and alcohol—and then not enforcing them. When athletes admit to a problem, or are caught abusing drugs, the coaches make allowances, give them second chances, accept excuses. The only result is that the problem gets worse, while the athletes are convinced that they can get away with any kind of misconduct.

Hall believes firmness is the only effective response. Coaches must set limits and stick to them. His own policy is simple. Athletes who turn themselves in are guaranteed that they will be kept on the team, that their problem will be kept strictly confidential, and that they will receive professional help. Athletes who try to conceal their drug abuse but are caught are off the team for the rest of the season. They will get professional help if they want it. There are no exceptions, ever.

When athletes have to be disciplined for violating training rules, they should know the coach will not reject them totally. They need his help to regain their youthful dignity and to get their lives back in order. Firmness, yes, but sympathy, too.

And then, there are the coaches who themselves drink. They indulge heavily at athletic clinics, during summer activities, at adult parties, at victory celebrations, or when drowning their sorrows over a lost game. That kind of behavior is hard to hide. Some coaches hardly bother. There are those who seem to think it amusing to joke with their players, or brag to them, about their drinking prowess. Such men are hardly the role models their young charges need.

What can coaches do to discourage rather than encourage drug and alcohol abuse? Hall offers many suggestions.

They can call their team captains together early and often, to discuss the drug problem. They can get the captains to work on their teammates, to persuade them to observe all training rules.

Hall urges coaches to "open a dialogue" with their athletes. They should be frank about any past or present drug or alcohol incidents on the team. The subject should be kept up front all season long. Once a week is the minimum.

Most importantly, coaches need to get their players to pressure each other to avoid drugs. Peer pressure is the key to success. Team members should confront users and say things like, "One more time and we turn you over to the coach," or, "I will do whatever it takes to get you to knock it off."

Instead of finding reasons to excuse abuser-athletes, coaches must have the courage to report all violations of training rules to the athletic director or school principal. That has to include violations by star players. Nothing destroys team morale more swiftly than athletes' perception that the rules apply to some but not to others.

Another effective technique that Hall uses in his school district is to get all athletes to sign cards in which they pledge to obey the rules. The cards are then mailed to their parents, who are asked to cosign them.

Programs like this one really do work. A survey taken after the first year in Hall's school district showed significant drops in athletes' drug and liquor abuse. Teams once riddled with drug problems were now clean.

Hall told of one female student's mother, who called the high school principal to complain that the coaches had ruined her daughter's party. They had urged the players not to attend because liquor would be served. "We were thrilled with that call," said Hall.

Hundreds of thousands of young Americans, Hall concluded, are "on a self-destructive course toward killing themselves." Adults—parents, teachers, coaches—dare not ignore this menace.

The most moving speech at the Long Beach conference was delivered by Carl Eller. A former All-Pro defensive end for the Minnesota Vikings, he played in four Super Bowls and was voted Most Valuable Player in two of them.

Eller was once a heavy drinker, a pot smoker, and a cocaine addict. When he retired from football, he became an NFL drug consultant. Eventually he worked out the league's antidrug program. Eller has helped many players hooked on drugs or liquor. For the past four years he has concentrated on working with teenagers. Eller says his antidrug efforts are his "5th Super Bowl."

He was in his early twenties when he was drafted by the Vikings, but he had been drinking for years. Still, he had never experienced anything like what he saw on the team. It had an unofficial motto: "If you want to be a Viking, you have to drink like a Viking!" Many of the players were proving their right to the title every day.

Eller eventually moved up to cocaine. It shortened his career, wrecked his personal life, and very nearly destroyed his health. One morning he looked in a mirror and couldn't recognize the drug-ravaged face that was staring back at him. That was the low point of his life, the shock that started him on the long painful climb back.

"What I needed," said Eller, "was someone to tell me no when I was a kid. I needed a role model. Kids still need that. I try to do what I can to fill the gap."

Eller admits that coaches acting individually cannot

achieve vast results in the war against drugs. But each of them can help save a few young people. And together, that can add up to a lot. It is a responsibility coaches cannot shirk.

The influence a coach can exercise over his players' use of drugs depends on his personal relationship with them. By treating them in a firm but friendly manner, avoiding the overused technique of shaming them when they make mistakes on the field, he can help build their egos. That will make it more likely that athletes will be willing to discuss their problems with him and to abide by his advice. It will also make it easier for them to turn down the frequent invitations they receive to share drugs with friends and teammates, or to accept them from others.

At the same time, coaches must bear in mind that they are not psychologists or social workers. They should not try to do jobs they are not trained for. When they become aware that a player has a drug or drinking problem, their proper role is to avoid criticism, be sympathetic and supportive, and encourage the player to accept professional counseling.

Newspaper headlines periodically reveal participation by coaches in recruitment cheating, secret payoffs to athletes, and other forms of corruption. In the immoral climate that such scandals promote, athletes can hardly help becoming cynical about the role of sports in society. If they then resort to drugs and drinking, they may feel their actions are no worse than those they see around them.

The cure for this problem is primarily in the hands of the coaches. Acting individually or through their organizations, they can root out those among them who betray their trust.

When prevention fails, and athletes fall victim to drugs, coaches have added responsibilities. They must be alert to significant changes in behavior and attitude. Some of the telltale signals include marked deterioration in an athlete's physical appearance or dress, missed practices, frequent lateness, lowered motivation and performance, involvement in fights and arguments, a shift to new and undesirable friends, defiant attitudes alternating with depression.

None of these prove the athlete is on drugs. They do indicate a need for the coach to talk with the athlete and offer help. The coach should maintain an up-to-date list of the sources of professional counseling. He should know the procedures for referring the athlete.

Just how badly lacking these skills are—at least among some coaches—was outlined in a notable statement by Federal judge Maurice Cohill, Jr., in November 1985. Cohill had just sentenced one of several drug dealers who had been selling cocaine to major-league baseball players in Pittsburgh. He expressed dismay over what he saw as "the managers' blindness to their players' personal and professional degeneration on the playing field and in the clubhouse." The judge felt strongly that "the owners should at least require their managers and coaches to get some professional training in spotting these problems."

PREVENTION FOR POLICYMAKERS

League officials, team owners, sports administrators, and others who set policy have the power to shape the environment that surrounds the world of athletics. Theirs is the primary responsibility for keeping sports clean.

Those who manage and administer sports are sometimes accused of caring more about their revenues and prestige than about their athletes. They can only refute this accusation by actions proving that they care genuinely about athletes' health and welfare.

Some of the policies already in effect in the major sports demonstrate this kind of concern. One is the rule that encourages drug-affected players to come forward voluntarily, without facing any threat of punishment. Otherwise, if athletes get the impression that the front office is seeking out drug abusers only to penalize them, they will hardly be likely to cooperate in programs designed to reduce the problem. Correctly or not, many athletes see demands for compulsory testing as targeted at them.

Vigorous enforcement of rules prohibiting injured athletes from being compelled to play would further enhance the reputations of those who run the sports enterprise.

Yet there has been little evidence so far of a spiteful attitude on the part of league officials and team managements. Players with drug or drinking habits have generally been treated leniently. In most cases, the teams have picked up the costs of treatment and rehabilitation, and have welcomed recovered players back. The teams' demand for mandatory testing may turn into an effective prevention step, if players' rights are safeguarded.

Another way to enlist the support of players is by giving them, or their elected representatives, a role in the development of antidrug policies and programs. The joint drug program in effect in the NBA since 1983 is an excellent model for this kind of cooperation.

At the college level, prevention measures have varied widely from one institution to another. It is true, however, that more colleges are offering drug education programs than ever before.

Overall responsibility for college athletics rests with the NCAA. Its recent adoption of a national drug-testing program was a major step forward that will doubtless help reduce the problem in the colleges. But the NCAA will have to strengthen its weak and ineffective enforcement arms.

A recent effort to make the NCAA more forceful was the formation of a Presidents' Commission, comprising the heads of member colleges and universities. These executives had formerly seemed content to leave sports policy in the hands of their athletic departments. Now they seem determined to take an active hand in cleaning up the corruption and the drug involvements that have dirtied college sports.

The Presidents' Commission has pushed the NCAA to adopt a number of major reforms. These include rigorous penalties for violations of the recruitment rules and raising the academic standards for athletes' admission to college, as well as the new national plan for drug testing.

The high schools, too, are expanding their antidrug efforts. Brice Durbin of the National Federation of State High School Associations recently said, "Enforcement does not reduce the problem. Education is the best way to go." His organization had started in the fall of 1984 with seminars on chemical health education. It hopes to expand with programs for coaches and high school officials as well as students. "We are going to be aggressive on this," Durbin pledged.

Perhaps the most extreme recommendation for dealing with the drug crisis is one that came from coach Frank Layden of basketball's Utah Jazz. "We need a security force," said Layden, "a central agency" to conduct the antidrug campaign in sports. It would "try to find the people selling the drugs to the players."

Layden reflected the feeling of most coaches and sports administrators when he added, "I'm usually against federal agencies involving themselves in sports." But, he concluded regretfully, the establishment of a powerful federal agency "is the only way to get teeth into the drug rules."

There is no doubt that periodic sports scandals—the flow of headlines about athletes caught using and dealing drugs—have caused some to doubt that sports authorities can solve the problem on their own. There have been persistent rumors of Congressional investigations. If these should happen, they might well produce legislation setting up a Federal bureaucracy to regulate sports.

That is a solution few in sports would welcome. There is still time to perfect alternative approaches. Some of these are already in place. A good beginning has been made.

America's athletes are only people. They live in society, not apart from it. The society they live in is more deeply infected by the drug plague every day. Antidrug programs will ease the problem, and must be tried. But the only realistic conclusion is that athletes will not conquer their drug problems until the rest of America does.

GLOSSARY

Most of the specialized terms used in this book have been explained in the text. This brief glossary may be helpful in understanding the few terms not fully defined.

Amphetamines. Pills taken for extra energy, confidence, and aggressiveness. Supposedly available only by a doctor's prescription. Usually sold under brand names such as Benzedrine, Dexedrine, and Dexamil. Popularly known as "uppers," "bennies," "pep pills," "greenies," "beans," and many other names.

Detoxification. The process of cleansing drugs or alcohol out of an addict's system.

Drug rehabilitation. The process of repairing mental and physical damage resulting from drug abuse, preparing the addict to resume normal living.

Freebasing. A method of treating cocaine so that it gives a more intense high. The user mixes the cocaine with ether, lighter fluid, or some other flammable substance. He then heats the mixture, obtaining a purified and more potent cocaine base.

Snorting. The most widely used method of taking cocaine. The user lays out the white powder in "lines" on some smooth surface. He then inhales one line at a time through any type of rolled paper. Or he may snort from a tiny "coke spoon."

Waive, waiver. When a team "waives" an athlete, it is giving up any claim it has on his services and making him available to any other team that may want him. Being waived is equivalent to being fired.

Withdrawal. The symptoms experienced by an addict when he stops drinking or taking drugs.

SUGGESTIONS FOR FURTHER READING

Information about some of the primary sources consulted for this book can be found in the Acknowledgments on pages vii–viii. The listing that follows is mainly comprised of secondary sources.

There exist very few previous works written especially for young readers on this subject. A few that deal with the drug problem in general have been included.

Other books with reading levels most nearly suitable for preteens and teenagers have been marked with an asterisk. Most of the listed biographies and periodical articles are fairly readable.

BOOKS

Berger, Gilda. *Addiction: Its Causes, Problems, and Treatment.* New York: Watts, 1982. For young adults.

Cohen, Miriam. *Marijuana: Its Effects on Mind and Body.* New York: Chelsea House, 1985. A study by a specialist in mind-altering drugs.

Dolan, Edward F., Jr. *Drugs in Sports.* New York: Franklin Watts, 1986. For younger readers.

Edwards, Harry. *Sociology of Sport.* Homewood, Ill.: Dorsey Press, 1973. A pioneering work by a black ex-athlete, now a prominent sociologist.

Forrest, Gary G. *How to Cope with a Teenage Drinker.* New York: Atheneum, 1983. Advice for adults.

*Gent, Peter. *North Dallas Forty.* New York: New American

Library, 1974. A football novel (and motion picture) that illustrates the use of drugs enabling injured athletes to "play with pain."

*Gold, Mark S. *800-Cocaine*. New York: Bantam, 1984. Dr. Gold is the founder of the national hot line for cocaine users.

Goldman, Bob, with Patricia Bush and Ronald Klatz. *Death in the Locker Room: Steroids and Sports*. South Bend, Ind.: Icarus Press, 1984. Massive study by a former weightlifter turned medical researcher.

*Goldstein, Jeffrey H., ed. *Sports Violence*. New York: Springer-Verlag, 1983. A useful anthology.

Halberstam, David. *The Breaks of the Game*. New York: Knopf, 1981. A writer follows the Portland Trail Blazers through a season.

Hyde, Margaret O., ed. *Mind Drugs*. New York: McGraw-Hill, 1981. Anthology for early teens.

Isaacs, Neil D. *Jock Culture, U. S. A.* New York: Norton, 1978. A university professor describes his encounters with athletes in a sports literature course.

Koppett, Leonard. *Sports Illusion, Sports Reality*. Boston: Houghton-Mifflin, 1981. Criticism of the sports establishment by a columnist.

Lapchick, Richard. *Broken Promises: Racism in American Sports*. New York: St. Martin's/Marek, 1984. The jarring story of a white professor who tried to fight race prejudice.

Lukas, Scott E. *Amphetamines: Danger in the Fast Lane*. New York: Chelsea House, 1985. Points up the risks.

Madison, Arnold. *Drugs—and You*. Rev. ed. New York: Messner, 1982. For preteens.

Mandell, Arnold. *The Nightmare Season*. New York: Random House, 1976. A psychiatrist recalls a wrenching year as counselor to a pro football team.

*Michener, James. *Sports in America.* New York: Random House, 1976. Detailed analysis by one of America's most popular novelists.

Mirkin, Gabe. *The Sportsmedicine Book.* Boston: Little, Brown & Co., 1978. Packed with sound information.

*O'Brien, Robert, and Sidney Cohen. *The Encyclopedia of Drug Abuse.* New York: Facts on File, 1984. Informative, comprehensive, and readable.

Ogilvie, Bruce, and Thomas Tutko. *Problem Athletes and How to Handle Them.* London: Pelham Books, 1966. Revealing and still relevant insights by two distinguished psychologists.

Schwarzrock, Shirley, and C. Gilbert Wrenn. *Facts and Fantasies about Drugs.* Circle Pines, Minn.: American Guidance, 1970. Accurate information for teenagers.

Scott, Jack. *The Athletic Revolution.* New York: Free Press, 1971. An early radical critique of the sports system.

Stone, Nannette, Marlene Fromme, and Daniel Kagan. *Cocaine: Seduction and Solution.* New York: Crown, 1984. Scientific data and recommendations for treatment.

Straub, William F., ed. *Sport Psychology: An Analysis of Athlete Behavior.* Ithaca, N.Y.: Movement Publications, 1978. Perceptive essays.

Talamini, John T., and Charles H. Page, eds. *Sport and Society: An Anthology.* Boston: Little, Brown & Co., 1973. Essays that put sport in perspective.

Taylor, William N. *Anabolic Steroids and the Athlete.* Jefferson, N.C.: McFarland, 1982. A maverick physician takes issue with the medical establishment.

————. *Hormonal Manipulation: A New Era of Monstrous Athletes.* Jefferson, N.C.: McFarland, 1985. Even-handed presentation of the steroid problem.

Teenagers Themselves, compiled by the *Glenbord East Echo.*

New York: Adama Books, 1984. Candid revelations by high school students on many topics including drugs and drinking.

*Underwood, John. *The Death of an American Game: The Crisis in Football.* Boston: Little, Brown & Co., 1979. A leading sportswriter urges reform.

*————. *Spoiled Sport: A Fan's Notes on the Troubles of Spectator Sports.* Boston: Little, Brown & Co., 1984. The writer extends his critique to the entire field of sports.

*Yeager, Robert C. *Seasons of Shame: The New Violence in Sports.* New York: McGraw-Hill, 1979. Investigation of an increasingly serious problem.

BIOGRAPHIES

Abdul-Jabbar, Kareem, and Peter Knobler. *Giant Steps: The Autobiography of Kareem Abdul-Jabbar.* New York: Bantam, 1983. Basketball's all-time greatest.

Ashe, Arthur. *Advantage Ashe.* New York: Coward-McCann, 1967. First black tennis champion.

Bouton, Jim. *Ball Four Plus Ball Five.* New York: Stein and Day, 1981. Updated version of a baseball best-seller.

Bradley, Bill. *Life on the Run.* New York: Quadrangle/New York Times Book Co., 1976. Former basketball superstar, now a U.S. senator.

Cosell, Howard. *I Never Played the Game.* New York: Morrow, 1985. Hard-hitting memoirs of the celebrated TV sportscaster.

Hernandez, Keith, and Mike Bryan. *If at First: A Season with the Mets.* New York: McGraw-Hill, 1986. Star first baseman beats cocaine addiction.

Kramer, Jerry. *Instant Replay: The Green Bay Diary of Jerry Kramer.* New York: New American Library, 1968. Longtime best-seller by key player in a Super Bowl team.

Meggysey, Dave. *Out of Their League.* Palo Alto, Calif.: Ramparts Press, 1970. One of the earliest exposés of pro football, by a respected player.

Porter, Darrell, and William Deerfield. *Snap Me Perfect: The Darrell Porter Story.* New York: Nelson, 1983. A catcher who overcame multiple addictions.

Ralbovsky, Martin. *The Namath Effect.* Englewood Cliffs, N.J.: Prentice-Hall, 1976. The colorful quarterback known as Broadway Joe.

Russell, Bill, and Taylor Branch. *Second Wind: The Memoirs of an Opinionated Man.* New York: Random House, 1979. No-holds-barred reminiscences of one of basketball's first black superstars.

Welch, Bob, with George Vecsey. *Five O'Clock Comes Too Early: A Young Man's Struggle with Alcoholism.* New York: William Morrow, 1982. A pitcher conquers his self-destructive weakness.

PAMPHLETS

American Civil Liberties Union. *Drug Testing in the Workplace.* New York: American Civil Liberties Union, 1986.

Committee on Substance Abuse Research and Education. *USOC Drug Control Program: Questions and Answers.* Colorado Springs, Colo.: U.S. Olympic Committee, 1985. Information for Olympic athletes.

Controlled Substances: Use, Abuse, and Effects. Washington, D.C.: Drug Enforcement Administration, 1984. Fact-filled four-page folder.

Deighan, William P., Michael D. Hall, Peg Rider. *Team Up for Drug Prevention with America's Young Athletes.* Washington, D.C.: Drug Enforcement Administration, 1984. Model program for drug abuse prevention in the schools.

For Coaches Only: How to Start a Drug Prevention Program. Washington, D.C.: Drug Enforcement Administration, 1984. Practical advice.

Griffin, Thomas M. *Paying the Price.* Center City, Minn.: Hazelden Foundation, 1985. The pressures on athletes, with suggested ways of coping.

Svendsen, Roger, Thomas M. Griffin, and Dorothy E. McIntyre, eds. *Chemical Health: School Athletics and Fine Arts Activities.* Center City, Minn.: Hazelden Foundation, 1984. Drug problems in schools, with suggested remedial strategies.

PERIODICALS

"Athletes and Their 'Recreational Drugs,' " *U.S. News and World Report,* October 17, 1983. How addictions start.

Anderson, Ian. "Drugs and the Olympics: Controversies Over Use and Detection," *World Press Review,* March 1984. Unsettled international issues.

Brubaker, Bill. "Bittersweet," *Sports Illustrated,* February 4, 1985. Basketball player's fight against cocaine addiction.

———. "A Pipeline Full of Drugs," *Sports Illustrated,* January 21, 1985. Exposé of drug trafficking in sports.

"Cashing In on Heavy Checking," *Psychology Today,* November 1979. Hockey violence.

Clarke, Kenneth S. "The Dope on Drug Control," *Womensports,* July 1984. Recommendations by director of sports medicine for U.S. Olympic Committee.

Cosell, Howard, Harry Edwards, Billie Jean King, Robert Lipsyte, Digger Phelps, George Plimpton, Tom Sanders, David J. Stern. "Sports: How Dirty A Game?" *Harper's Magazine,* September 1985. Lively discussion by noted sports figures.

Cramer, Richard Ben. "Olympic Cheating: The Inside Story of Illicit Doping and the U.S. Cycling Team," *Rolling Stone,* February 14, 1985. Blood-packing scandal.

Edwards, Harry. "The Black 'Dumb Jock': An American Sports Tragedy," *College Board Review,* Spring 1984. Critique of treatment of black athletes by schools and colleges.

———. "Educating Black Athletes," *The Atlantic,* August 1983. Recommendations for reform.

Exley, Frederick. "Sidelines," *Rolling Stone,* September 15, 1983. Drugs in football.

Franks, Lucinda. "A New Attack on Alcoholism," *New York Times Magazine,* October 20, 1985. New scientific discoveries.

Gilbert, Bill. "Drugs in Sport," *Sports Illustrated,* June 23, June 30, July 7, 1969. Early investigative report.

Gomez, Linda. "Cocaine: America's 100 Years of Euphoria and Despair," *Life,* May 1984. Spectacularly illustrated historical review.

Hamilton, Jonathan. "Who Are the Steroid Pushers?" *Womensports,* October 1983. Accuses coaches, trainers, team physicians.

Hill, Henry, and Douglas S. Looney. "How I Put the Fix In," *Sports Illustrated,* February 16, 1981. Gambler bribes Boston College basketball players.

Hopkins, Thomas. "Playing Football Under a Snowdrift," *MacLeans,* June 21, 1982. Cocaine epidemic.

"How Drugs Threaten to Ruin Pro Sports," *U.S. News and World Report,* September 12, 1983. The mounting crisis.

Jones, David A., and Leverett T. Smith, Jr., eds. "Sports in America," *Journal of Popular Culture,* Spring 1983. Entire issue devoted to sports problems.

Kane, Martin. "An Assessment of 'Black is Best,' " *Sports Illustrated,* January 18, 1971. Debatable explanation of black superiority in sports.

Kaplan, Jim. "Taking Steps to Solve the Drug Dilemma," *Sports Illustrated,* May 28, 1984. Suggestions for reform.

————, and Ivan Maisel. "The Commissioner Gets Tough," *Sports Illustrated,* May 20, 1985. Mandatory testing issue in baseball.

Kaufman, Irving R. "The Battle over Drug Testing," *New York Times Magazine,* October 19, 1986. A defense of testing.

Kranzley, Glenn. "Treating Olympic Injuries: New Drug-Free Alternatives for All Riders," *Bicycling,* May 1984. Progress in sports medicine.

Lamar, Jacob V., Jr. "Scoring Off the Field," *Time,* August 25, 1986. How and why the problem is worsening throughout sports.

Lieber, James. "Coping with Cocaine," *The Atlantic,* January 1986. Recommends involuntary commitment of addicts.

Lipsyte, Robert. "Baseball and Drugs," *The Nation,* May 25, 1985. Author and TV sports commentator challenges official policy on drug testing.

Looney, Douglas S. "A Test with Nothing But Tough Questions," *Sports Illustrated,* August 9, 1982. Testing issue in pro football.

Maisel, Ivan. "The Stuff I Did Was Enough to Kill You," *Sports Illustrated,* May 28, 1984. Athlete's addiction story.

Neff, Craig. "Caracas: A Scandal and a Warning," *Sports Illustrated,* September 5, 1983. Crackdown on drugs in international competition.

Neff, Craig, and Robert Sullivan. "The NFL and Drugs," *Sports Illustrated,* February 10, 1986. The worsening situation in pro football.

Ogilvie, Bruce, and Thomas A. Tutko. "Sport: If You Want to Build Character, Try Something Else," *Psychology Today,* October 1971. Refutes widely held assumptions.

Rashad, Ahmad. "Journal of a Plagued Year," *Sports Illustrated,* October 18, 1982. Pro football star's revelations.

Reese, Don, and John Underwood. "I'm Not Worth A Damn," *Sports Illustrated,* June 14, 1982. Exposé of widespread drug abuse in National Football League.

Rozelle, Pete, and Peter Ueberroth. "Talking Sports," *New York Times Magazine,* October 6, 1985. National Football League and major league baseball commissioners discuss common problems.

Sanoff, Alvin P. "Drug Problems in Athletics: It's Not Only the Pros," *U.S. News and World Report,* October 17, 1983. Spread of the drug epidemic to younger athletes.

"Sports Gambling" (series of five articles), *Sports Illustrated,* March 10, 1986. Eye-opening exploration of an expanding menace.

"STH: The Secret Steroid," *Sport,* February 1984. Human growth hormones.

Todd, Terry. "The Steroid Predicament," *Sports Illustrated,* August 1, 1983. Warning by former weightlifting champion.

————. "The Use of Human Growth Hormone Poses Grave Dilemmas for Sport," *Sports Illustrated,* October 15, 1984. The warning elaborated.

Wade, Nicholas. "Anabolic Steroids: Doctors Denounce Them, But Athletes Aren't Listening," *Science,* June 1972. Sports physician on steroid side effects.

Will, George F. "Exploring the Racer's Edge," *Newsweek,* February 4, 1985. Performance boosters.

INDEX

187